A BIRD BLACK AS THE SUN

A BIRD BLACK AS THE SUN

California Poets on Crows & Ravens

Edited by
Enid Osborn and Cynthia Anderson

Green Poet Press
2011

© 2011 by Enid Osborn and Cynthia Anderson

All rights reserved. No portion of this work may be reproduced or transmitted in any form without permission in writing from Green Poet Press.

Green Poet Press is affiliated with Green Poet Project, founded in 1999 by Enid Osborn to promote spoken word events and small poetry publications in Santa Barbara, California and surrounding areas.

ISBN: 978-0-615-53632-3

Front cover woodcut: "Raven" by Lisa Brawn
Back cover woodcut: "Raven Calling" by Lisa Brawn
Crow silhouettes, cover and interior: Amy Floyd
Illustration opposite title page: "Heading In" by Amy Floyd

Cover and Interior Design: Margy Brown Design, Santa Barbara, California

Orders, inquiries, and correspondence should be addressed to:
Green Poet Press
P.O. Box 6927
Santa Barbara, CA 93160
www.greenpoetpress.com

Raven
on a roost of furs
No bird in a bird-book,
black as the sun.

— Gary Snyder,
from *Myths and Texts*

TABLE OF CONTENTS

JOKER

MESSENGER

NIGHT-BRINGER

Editors' Note

In February 2010, word spread quickly about the "Crow Talk!" reading in Goleta, California. Poets and poetry-lovers descended for a lively afternoon of spoken word hosted by Green Poet Project. A recording of crows' voices filled the hall as the crowd gathered. Shortly, crows began their evening migration over the old Union School, as readers rolled out inspired poems — their own and the work of others — about those most provocative birds.

The exuberance of that reading, and the resulting clamor for more opportunities to share poetry about crows and ravens, led to the idea for a book. A statewide call for submissions ensued, followed by a year of thoughtful collaboration as this anthology took shape.

We would like to extend special thanks to Margy Brown Design of Santa Barbara, to our spouses for their unflagging support, and especially to all of the poets who submitted their work. One characteristic that sets corvidae apart from other birds is their ability to individuate and surprise. We could say the same about the California poets who fill these pages.

We hope this anthology gives you, the reader, caws to celebrate.

Enid Osborn and Cynthia Anderson

Awakener

Lawrence Ferlinghetti

IN WOODS WHERE MANY RIVERS RUN

In woods where many rivers run
                      among the unbent hills
     and fields of our childhood
                       where ricks and rainbows mix in memory
although our 'fields' were streets
              I see again those myriad mornings rise
    when every living thing
                  cast its shadow in eternity
    and all day long the light
                 like early morning
   with its sharp shadows shadowing
                   a paradise
      that I had hardly dreamed of
                 nor hardly knew to think
    of this unshaved today
               with its derisive rooks
  that rise above dry trees
             and caw and cry
and question every other
         spring and thing

Jim Natal

EARLY MORNING CROW

Crows have no shame. They caw at 6 A.M.,
expect a response from windows reflecting
overcast skies, wait for an echo
to return across the canyon, for the bottle
to wash up on shore, the telephone
to ring, the empty half of the bed to fill.
                                    You cannot throw
a boot at them like sex-struck cartoon cats
yowling backlit by the moon, cannot
shoo them like pie-faced pasture cows ruminating
with the intensity of low-watt bulbs.
                                    The crows wake you
too early. And there you are, an overdue
bill, over-ripe melon, alone with your thoughts sluicing
back through the gates you had to lower by hand
the night before, cranking rusty cogs and wheels
so you could get some sleep.
                                    The bed floods
and you rise, afloat with black wings spread
like oil upon the surface, a near-fatality
the cold almost got, wet through and hearing
a solitary crow that croaks:
                        Is anybody there?
                        Is anybody there?
then flies away before you can form
                        a suitable answer.

Susan Kelly-DeWitt

CONFRONTING THE ANGEL

Crow's cawing wakes
even the sleepers,
who stream out from their blue

houses to hear his prickly
dream of leaves.
What does he think

of our world, high up
on his needled peak?
Together we look out

at the streets —
harbinger, nether one,
and I, who have come

wearing my white
apron, intending to empty
a sack of trash.

Suddenly
I am chef
of the morning!

I dare to show him
the flour on my fingers
and the knife.
The knife!

Edwin Shaw

CROW SONG

This morning, before dawn, something got these crows worked up,
and now they are wheeling above me, talking trash and telling lies
with all of the pretensions of the devil's own stallions
stampeding across the black asphalt pavement of the sky.

Like a night of left-handed angels, the raucous crows descend
and brag about their petty crimes, their tattoos and addictions;
this flock of happy sociopaths, gathering on a corner,
intimidates the frightened shadows into a vague extinction.

Laughing like cold, black flames, these crows, these wannabe gangsters,
more like undertakers now, at the troubled edge of sleep,
where they poke through Love's vacant lots, looking for my broken heart
among the rotting garbage dumped from last night's hobo feast.

I don't know, maybe it's strange, but I have always liked these crows,
I've found them smart, like little Charlie Chaplin in his worn frock coat,
they are ultimately comical, self-assured, a little maniacal,
and when they walk, they walk like pirates or like Buddhist monks.

But smelling of smoke this morning and gleaming with a blue-black sheen,
like pieces of charred wood flung across the sky's cold, blank shell,
these crows, in their stately pantomime, fly across my dreams
and now in January's harsh winter light, I know they've been to hell.

Like the worn-out memories of once proud, fallen angels,
these crows, perched in the leafless trees, attempt an evil song,
but lacking in the grandeur of true romantic badness,
they croak out dull melodies now that merely annoy the dawn.

Mary Kay Rummel

WINTER MORNING WITH CROW

At the first stroke of sunlight you're at it
haranguing me with your vivid
monosyllabic. You land and strut
in the street —Tut's heir or Napoleon's —

You probably have taken Russia.
This is your season. You like glitter,
ice-thin skins on the walks,
bare branches paring a wan sky.

No better perch to show you off.
There's nothing you want more
than to be seen unless it's to be heard
as you are telling me now.

You cock your head at me
your feathery dark
which deforms into flight
leaves the oak branch shaking.
One black feather sears
my backyard stretch of snow.

Christopher Buckley

CROWS IN COATESVILLE

With morning's first metallic shimmer of the light, they shake loose
from their cacophonous boughs,

and though I'm lying calm as fog over the lake of sleep, they cruise
lowly by, their din and yaws

cutting in with a *Chris, Chris, Chris* as they take up their icy stations
in the air. And over the smoke-

smudged trestle and the mill, a rancor rings against the restoration
of our world as if hills of ash and oak

were still all theirs. They line out like sutures on the sky and bivouac
refuting the frosted blue

as evidence that none of this will tell on their oiled and easy backs,
saying, *We were here before you,*

will be here when you're gone. The graveyard is the one cleared space
along the ridge and sundown wields

its copper swath across the runted stones, brazing the heart-shaped face
of a monument at once annealed

to light — above it, they'll weave out and back, reconnoiter on dusk's last
glassy span before they settle

in to roost, but first they spiral skyward like burning flakes of trash
from an open fire, and pepper

the raw air down which we hear the wind and sawtoothed whisper
of their wings. They do this

in case their meaning might be overlooked, or we're consoled by winter's
choir of clouds; my friend insists

that from where they sit they wish us death, knew this as a boy when
they strafed his father's bed

of white seraphic roses, diving from their republic of broken limbs
to clip the milky heads.

Self-conscious symbols, yet each night they're more than content to be
shining with doubt like black sparks,

like swart blossoms clotted and fixed above us in the leaf-bare trees
as they sound out the dark.

— for Tim Geiger

Abigail Brandt

I'm Listening, Crow

I'm listening, crow,
as your gravel clatter
rasps the silence of dawn.
Jar me back from
unholy dreams,

awaken me early,
though my eyes
are still too asleep
to discern
the nacreous light of day.

Jangle and jeer
your invisibility,
perhaps from the forest
of ghost trees
out in back.

You never come near.
You are too wild
a trickster to feed
alongside finches and wrens.
Bringer of change,

scold my hidden lesson
to every direction,
expose me to every wind.
Unctuous omen,
messenger bird,

your coal black feathers
sketch the nuance
between shadow and light.
Shifter of shapes,
heal me, reveal me.

What bright fob
dangles from your beak?
You from the void
between worlds,
you with no sense of time.

Constance Crawford

LIFTOFF

This morning, the crows are noisy
outside our still-dim bedroom.
A racket of warnings, gripes and ridicule —
every crow adds to it as they wake and fly.
Curled, eyes sealed, I ache from the hard old mattress.
Out there, they stretch and fan the fresh dawn air.
Predators, omnivores, junk food addicts,
they thrive. Our local chapter of the Crow Club swells
in its redwood headquarters above the football field.
Just let the dainty bushtit try to raise a brood!
Yet, my heart wants curing from yesterday's stale quarrel,
so why not let them —
compromised, garrulous gorgers that they are —
lift me toward today's conceivable happiness?

ENIGMA

Michael Hannon

BORN AGAIN

You can't trust oblivion.

In The Serious Mountains,
a hidden lake, utterly still
is swept suddenly by rain.

Crow hops out of no crow
and eats the diamond —
countless births, countless deaths.

Sky brims over with sky,
Wind harrows the grasses,
River narrows and quickens,
stronger than the strongest swimmer.

It's only March, and already
the pear blossoms are falling.

Just remember this —
you weren't the one
who wanted to be a separate being.

You are the frail wing, rescuing love
from love's faceless mirror.

Patrick Daly

ANOTHER CROW

It lifted from a branch and flew
and settled. How black it shone against the grey
of not-yet-spring, stark
as the bare tree. For a wingbeat
I felt myself pitching into crow,
all the not enough that is bird in me wanting
to fan out into black,
to feel the inklings of blackness
prickle my veins, while a black beak began
to refine my bones.
How strong
longing is. I was willing to let go
and take that coal-bright, prying grip upon the world
just to cross the road in one beat and glide,
to stretch wings at the tips like aching fingers
and stall and settle. For three moments of flight
I would have ceased this human leaning into otherness
and leapt into crow forever.
And though I was not bird enough, too much a man
waiting for a bus under low clouds,
I felt my balance dip crow-ward by a feather, a tickle
of black brilliance, something light
as a shadow cross my heart.

Maia

LIGHT-CATCHER

Under her breast the land is passing
and the dune-rivers run

through the hands of gravity and wind sings like
mist off the sinusoidal
spine and the sidewinding fluent traces

and the ramified rootworks of
grasses clinging to temporary mountains

Raven   light-catcher   sees desert full of bones
and premonitions   a vast soul crooked
deceiving in fleeting hospitable

shifts of light   feeding her eye
sharp as cactus   tough as rock   tender-hearted
as a cloud that escapes

with a bellyful of rain into the next state
and breaks into a fountain
upside down in the sky

Dan Gerber

THE CROW

I am walking on the Earth, held down
by the specifics of everything
around me. Things circle, though I don't quite
perceive them as moving, except of course
the crow making lazy swats at the moment
through which he swims like a lumbering skate.

He flaps on beyond the bend of the planet,
or beyond the canyon's pine ridge
where I can no longer see him
and assume he's a prophet now, living in Judaea,
preaching to a glade in Ninevah.

Sylvia Alcon

MEDITATION HALL

Just sit,
the kindly monk instructs and, eyes cast down,
I join the silent, dark-robed monks sitting cross-legged
on their cushions. Perched on a square black pillow,
my mind flutters, pecks at juicy insect thoughts,
yawns, and cawing, flies out through the window
to join crows on the phone wires where they just sit.

Len Anderson

ON THE NATURE
OF THINGS

The squawking crow
flies down from the redwood tree
to tell me
he is not a crow.

Not bird, not passerine bird
of the family *Corvidae*,
nor mind nor body
nor thing.

And not a crow.

In fact, he says,
he hasn't even been
discovered yet.

When I was young, I dreamt
I climbed marble stairs
toward the room that held
The Book of What Each Thing Is.
Golden light poured down those stairs
from a room so high
I could never see it.

From that book
I would learn
what is *crow*,
what is *redwood*,
what am I.

Crow tells me
the black of his wings
is deeper than any book.

Friends, there are hours
I have no greater grief,
no greater joy.

I will never know
what I am.

Crow
flies down often
to tell me so.

R. S. Read

TRUE TONGUES

At sunset, crows perch in the pines like open mouths,
Make catcalls at the solitary buck, antlers swathed in green pelage,
Who stretches his neck into the shaggy scrub.

Crow, buck, open mouths — names that are not forever —
Like boundary stones from a vanished empire,
Each sits upon a shelf above its label.

It is our fate to name debris from the ancient star
Whose seeds flower in the full moon cameo,
In ebony wings and in hooves that scrape the dusty hills,

Those wings shaped by solar wind that drove them,
Minds molded around the voids
That held them in their sailing.

Whenever one speaks, ten thousand words stand up,
Point to a tower unfurling like an endless exhalation,
All existence engraved on every single one.

William Everson (Brother Antoninus)

THESE ARE THE RAVENS

These are the ravens of my soul,
Sloping above the lonely fields
And cawing, cawing.
I have released them now
And sent them wavering down the sky,
Learning the slow witchery of the wind,
And crying on the farthest fences of the world.

MUSE

M. L. Brown

WHEATFIELD WITH CROWS
— after Vincent Van Gogh

He lays my bones on canvas, plays
the angles. The long ones he strokes
into stalks of wheat, ribs
into ruts and hillocks.
He ticks the short into storm.

I ride the rust of the road,
glim the green as it plows through.
My pale eyes mismatch
in the sky.

Then the crows tip in:
the troubles of heaven on the wing.

They do not consider the scare in me —
carved into cobalt, lucid in gold.
A man could die happily here.

Kit Kennedy

LICENSE TO TRAVEL

The boy's hand releases crows
folded precisely. Between fingers
paper is time, exploration
of the untested.

Flight happens without knowledge
of thermodynamics, ornithology.
No experience with compass
because he has no fear

that ground is failure. He came out
of the ground of his mother.

Simple, the pattern. Arc. Descent.
The absence of light across light.

He tells no one
where he and the crows have been.

Paula C. Lowe

SWARMING THE BOY, 1997

My side of the house, I heard the interchange, truckers
downshifting and homecomers slamming on brakes.

But from his bedroom, no matter the window open or closed,
crows ganged up on the boy's sleep, squatted on the roof outside

his bunk bed, cawing about raccoons taking crayfish,
cawing about juveniles who wouldn't take flight, cawing

while rain suppressed their feathers and left them stranded on this
patch of sheet asphalt, in this wooded cul-de-sac, in this town

north of a big city, and that boy tossed and turned, asked what
was the use of sleep with that gang chaining him to their gossip?

And I at my kitchen beaters didn't say, while he at our piano
sent his fingers flying over the octaves, basking on the black keys.

Diane Kirsten Martin

BIRD THROUGH FRAMES

Framed by the window, a raven
soars and sweeps in hale November.

The piano's *andante moderato* creates
another frame. We watch, expect

the bird to land on the English holly,
gravid with berries, but it circles

the tree, opens out to a spiral, flips,
coming round for another pass. The piece

shifts into *allegro*, the raven whips
and slides, and when the music turns

again — *meno mosso* — dips and swings
back up to a stately *ritardando*.

The piano silences. We turn back
to chores, the bird to its own music.

Bettina T. Barrett

A PASSING FEAST

I met a thoughtful raven
hand carved in wood and
placed on the windowsill
in a full summer's light

Raven stood quietly and
never moved   not even
when I came near to look
at feathers and that eye

Raven's beak was thick
and curved just so
shaped for the ease
of rounding up a passing feast

color was black but with red
purple   bits of blue
and gold-swept feathers
a sheen across the body

to reach and touch
was a wish denied   instead
I picked up pencil and paper
used what eyes could see and know

as thoughts slid over Raven's sleek
so immediate so ready for
the hand that could hold and carry
the distance from there to here

Charlotte Muse

WHO KNOWS CROW?

Not the tame hawk, fierce and embarrassed, leashed to a wrist,
nor the wild one on the air like Jesus on the water.
Not the seed eaters always looking down not the singers
holding up their throats.

To get to the bottom of crow,
you must look out of dark and chuckle.
Know yourself alone. Know yourself
smarter than some.

Draw a line in your mind from here
to there, and get there fast.
Don't be blinded by silver streamers
tied to the grape vines. Go on in.
What can they do about it?
What can they do about you?

Bad boy, joke joy, lover of the wind,
crow tries to connect.
He thinks things to himself,
flying over the cul-de-sacs.
He keeps a weather eye.

A landscape of crow would be
large in the tree,
small like ground pepper over the cornfield,
two bird-shadow hands in flight.

I wish I had the art to make mixed light
out of darkness, but when I look at what's moving,
I see crow, singing *harsh, harsh,* in the ice-crack voice
looking heavier than he is at the top of the tree
where there ought to be light.

If I were God, once I'd made crow and knew
he was a miracle, I'd want to make more.

ellen

GIVING BIRTH TO RAVENS

The woman lies on a bed of leaves
and waits for rain, suspended
in some pre-natural state, surviving
on moisture gathered from air.
Her body, dressed in weavings of grass,
is nested by the earth. She doesn't know
of having given birth to ravens,
but listens to their calls
until a man commands her to rise.
Like a sleepwalker,
she boards a train between 46th and 47th.
Her cool eyes reach out
among faces to be reckoned with.
She startles commuters as she comments
about something fluttering inside her.
Her hair bears the look of ruffled feathers,
her mouth the color of ripe currants.
She will crack new life open in her palm.

Doris Vernon

CROW AND THE ARTIST

Crow flings his black cloak over his bony shoulders
As he caws into the sky
He calls others from the Crow Clan
And leads them in a surveillance foray
Over the wheatfield
He's painting   He's painting   Look
They feel the vibrations rising through the layers of air
They watch the artist stagger through the field
Down the country road
Back to his hotel
Crow flaps back to his perch
And shivers as fingers of heat point at him.

Noreen Lawlor

TEMPO

I am a crow grown tired of my
wings
beating the vastness of sky
under them
I want to be of earth of the
cringing soil
and the scalding bones of men
I want to be of darkness not of
feathers
no longer fill my nest
with shiny things
rings from cracker jack boxes
it is the time
of hair and hands and blue eyes

Jackson Wheeler

CROW SINGS JAZZ

Who is to say that a crow which uses tools
Might not one day stand at a microphone
On a slow Sunday afternoon
In a bar where a piano
Plays the standards,
Given a steady diet of quarters?

Preen, preen, preen
Imagine Billie Holiday after the heroin
Kicked in — smooth, smooth
Imagine Nina Simone after she arrived in Paris
Medgar Evers' blood splattered all over her imagination
Finding something in the moment. . .

Safe, safe, safe
Among people who don't know the word *nigger*
It takes a lot of weed to get a voice that smooth
But a voice can be smooth and hard
Jazz needs sometimes to be hard
because it is the music that fits this world —

Music twisted like a twig in the anthill of the brain
A twig in the beak of a crow watching another crow
And another crow, and another, drawing
Out the contents it took a lifetime to preserve
Then feasting on what clings to all that memory
Music which is neither sad nor happy

It just is
Miles, Coltrane, that crazy gypsy guitarist, Django,
Cab Calloway over the top — not jazz, just approaching it
At the speed of music at the speed of the world
Turning itself upside down where jazz, we hope, is an antidote
But isn't — get that notion out of your head

What crows bring
From the feathered kingdoms of Heaven
Is an idea, offered by the likes of Billie and Nina
Singing all bold
And bright, voices preening
Made known in the world, smooth, smooth

If this is home, it is temporary
Anyplace is temporary that would allow a crow
On a Sunday afternoon to drop the twig of sustenance
And reach for the elixir of the microphone
To belt out a litany of sultry
Lyrics for a world going and gone

BELOVED

Lara Gularte

FINDING THE SACRED

Born with question marks
about my past,
my people,
I step inside myself
and find running water,
stones too heavy to bring up.
These waters fill the banks
with gold dust and granite,
shining mica and quartz.
No heaven here, but root,
alluvial and veined.
Still I hear voices,
see ghosts drift in and out,
the drone of the river.

In the old growth forest
I listen for footsteps
and hear birdsong.
In this place of rest,
this ancestral path of migration,
the air pulses angelic
from the throat of a sparrow.
In my hands, the smell of prayer
gathered in a bouquet of lavender.
Madrone bark,
red and gold,
flames like candles.
Crows on the church roof,
a ring of ancestors chanting.

Molly Fisk

SINGING CANYON SONNET

I have to say something about the blue grasses by the side of the road,
the red rock rising behind them, a lacy kind of scrub juniper,
yellow-green in afternoon light, dotted here and there up the broken slope

and walls scraped sheer, the red striated with bars of gold and brown.
I have to tell how two greasy ravens, startled from their perch,
made a raucous noise in the slot canyon. Their cries bounced upward,

magnified by a hundred where I had just been singing Amazing Grace,
the only hymn whose verses I reliably remember, and they had not stirred.
My boots raised puffs of fine red dust behind me walking back to the car.

I should mention that the aspen leaves were thumbnail-sized and vivid,
that anvil clouds quickly overtook the sun, that before I saw those thirty-seven
white-tailed deer I was feeling unbearably lonely, and I might as well confess

how acutely I miss the man I left at home, even though I drove
two thousand miles away from him to figure out which one of us to love.

Ruth Nolan

DESERT HOME DIASPORA
— to Phil Phonics

If you could call me one more time,
I'd say I'm looking at a raven sky,

that the California desert isn't Israel,
but our constellations are the same,

I'd say I'm overjoyed by pink
wildflower clouds in the garden, it's

April, and the tiny green oranges
you fingered are still on the trees,

I'd say the dog I love is still
healing from his back injury,

that I made a bit of extra cash from
selling the didgeridoo and shotgun,

that the needled Palo Verde trees
are sprayed with yellow flowers,

that purple-throated Costa's hummingbirds
suckle white sugar syrup from my feeder,

that the sunflower seeds you scattered
with one toss of hand are now sprouting,

and the crows are occupying the tallest
palm, though you once beat them away,

that at night, I finger the cement bottom
in the black end of pool, I'm lying

on my back at water's edge, crying
stars, pretending I don't miss you.

Katie Goodridge Ingram

THE EYE IN THE BEAK OF THE MIND

A raven in a rusty cage alters
the light in the studio of my artist.
I want things the way they were —
flat canvases, colors and bodies
he contorts to form his truth, and
his ignorance of my desire.

White-smocked, he strides through stripes
of sun, the skin I want to know hidden
in gold corduroy. His fingers over mine.
The mug of wine smells always of
him, of paint, linseed oil and smoke.
"Meet 'Never,'" he says. "She talks."
He stands too close. Silence.

I've had birds. I've cooed and chirped
and called into crow-talking trees.
This one is no mirror for my song.
Still, I hold a finger out as if she'll smell me,
learn me, as if she'll hop right
through the wire, close her eyes,
nuzzle my jaw with her satin head.
"Maybe she won't talk today."

He smiles in his peculiar downdrawn way.
I want to kiss those contradictory
lips, press the hook of his nose into my
cheek, sure that, as he painted me hunkering
wide-eyed over his writhing body,
he would know how to ride the divide
and render me from girl to woman.

Never rises from her sullen hunch.
Cobalt, carmine kindle on her feathered black.
She growls like the tethered dog next door.
A real eye sees me, curves its thought
down the long bone of her beak,
enters me with a sudden thrust.

His smock, the mug, my cape — I spin
down the stairs like a dervish, wheeling
through trees, brushing off words,
"Mine! Mine!" cawing in my hair.

Maureen Alsop

CLEDONOMANCY, SLEEP IN THE RAVEN'S THROAT

divination by means of chance remarks that are spoken without premeditation

Stitch by stitch in the shore's seam I measured fog's rotation. Thick loaves of air rounded stone cliffs. Waves bit gulls in a loose crochet. As you plucked a clear path of allegiance into your small environs, the lesser nighthawk foraged under a streetlamp. Had you seen the faces of the holy? Had you overthrown what lifted you? For long hours I had been mending the black pages of water and the creases in the sand where you disappeared. From my sleep in the raven's throat I saw you walking in the sun. I have forgotten the depth of the lake. The liquor swill of reeds under your skin.

Mary Fitzpatrick

JOURNEY THROUGH NIGHT

L.A. to Oakland — Highway 5 — socked-in gauze — dustbowl days:
Here's how it looked on the prairie during that other collapse.
Drained, drilled, mined, milked — and before too long
It's gone. Settle the dust with vetch. Sprinkle that alkaline
Water. Wait for the Holy Spirit of Clouds to fill up the sky.
I'm leaving. It will take all the art in the world to undo
This bleak land. The ribbon unfurls, the high beams unwind
The road, a spool of black speed and wind, black speed
And wind   where only   wheeling   crows   succeed.

I navigate a map of sighs, sighs amplified
By the black road I chart the night long, *Beloved,*
To arrive at your door. Dive
At your door with coffee and crows,
Hauling the clouds, fat envelopes
Of tears, pulling the black
Rumbling clouds, unpacking hurt
Like shirts, unpacking
To dress you with words. When rain
Breaks I see you
As the crows see you: elated
And startled by love.

Patrice Vecchione

THE PERSIMMON TREE SPEAKS
TO THE RAVENS
— for Eleanor

If I didn't have my once-a-year flash of color,
if all of me weren't about ripening and fruition,
I'd wish for your shiny, year-round depth of hue.
If my life weren't enduringly rooted
beside the dance hall window,
I'd envy the innumerable destinations
you so loudly chatter about:
telephone wire across a busy intersection —
bright cars racing for the finish,
street lamp below which heady students
exchange ideas, a ship's mast seconds before departure
onto the thrashing, open sea.

The sweep of your flight flushes my cheeks.
We make good partners, ravens,
though it's always you who must choose me.
Even to sing I require wind,
but then my voice is only like a girl's skirts rustling
as she walks across the floor into some boy's arms,
while your song is an unrelenting cacophony.

Together we make a painting.
At the height of my glory, come late autumn,
you descend as a crowd upon me, settling your wings.

Gray daylight startles at the sight of us.
I stand straightest then, as when paired dancers
lean against the window, press their hot bodies close.
My orange globes fill you with longing,
fluttering my leaves till they fall.

Eat of me. Take your fill.

Lois Klein

AFTER THE WEDDING

Leaves hang like useless hands
from hushed November branches.
On the patio, bird seed thrown yesterday
dusts the cracks between bricks.

Crows feast, then lift like black
umbrellas flapping open.
A breeze crawls silent shadows
across the deserted walk.

Married — not a word I can say yet
in the same breath as *my son* —
my youngest, whose swaddled body
once slept curved into
the soft nest of my shoulder.

I can still hear him
in the wordless morning — his breath
like the whisper of wings.

One by one the children leave
with no more ado than the crows
rising and sailing
            tilted
                    beyond sight.

OMEN

Ron Alexander

THE FELLING

Lacerations on my forearms bear witness
to the ornamental plum tree's struggle
not to be downed. Deaf to the insistent uproar
of crows around me, too late I saw

the crown of thorns above my head was a house
of twigs and horsehair, still aloft, but atilt.
One speckled, teal-blue eggshell lay broken at my feet,
a dime of golden yolk pooled on rutted concrete.

Rochelle Arellano

MODERN

She had stopped believing
in omens, choosing instead to be
startled, then amused, by a raven,
clumsy over its dead, that she swerved
to avoid in the middle of the road.
The raven beat up to the wire
and swayed, raucous. Later,
through tears, troubled by dreams,
she would remember that the moon
had been visible, even at noon.
Magic at midnight lay thickly,
gathering dust over her iridescent
wings. Who remembered Aegypt
anymore, or how to weave gold from straw?
The raven in her mirror
mounted its prey with a flourish
of black satin flaps, the caw of a crone
tearing rag, rending flesh from bone.

Glenna Luschei

BIRD OF PARADOX

Raven, always an omen,
hovered over Earthquake Park
above the gorse and blackberry
bush.

When I told the children about the divorce
I felt the earth would collapse again
right there in Alaska.

Always an omen, Raven
told me glory ahead.
I said Trickster.

When I walked with their father
my wedding ring finger hurt.
Glory ahead.
How could that be true?

We slept in a tent
on Homer Spit, ate the silver
salmon our son caught.

He understood what was happening
and took my part. Raven guarded us
until we walked out

the other side of the tent
into the predicted glory.

I understand now why Raven
stole the sun. He kept it glowing
for us.

Carol Muske-Dukes

CROWS

They were not the messengers I'd expected.
Late at night, I stared at the moonlit photograph:
The bird's furtive yellow gaze bent back over its
Wing, beak clamped on a gold wedding band.

At dawn, I woke to my wedding rings beside me
In the bed, next to my naked hand. Thief! That
Ragged caw, turning one hand against the other.
A body winging over the temple of change — gold

Mouths mouthing the terrible — Vows: I spoke them.
Crows circle, harden the bond. See how
The high piracies of the sky turned imperative —
Sanctioned by me, my dream:
                    I stole the past that willingly from myself.

Kathleen McClung

NEPHEW, BLURRED

1
My sister, amused, photographs
a windmill without blades.
In the backseat
we listen to a crow,
and he tells me he hates them.
He tells me they bring
bad luck. I believe him.
He is matter-of-fact, eleven,
and last year
he swallowed a fistful of lithium.

Again this flatness settles in,
and it's clear I need
a larger language,
a lens less clouded
by my flimsy diplomacy.
It won't suffice
simply to list
the ugly, the incomplete
on this tour: useless landmarks,
a dark harbinger balanced on a branch.

2
I am looking for him,
but he is not
the boy in my dream.
"He's not here,"
some other child says,
pensive in a tub
of warm water.

I am looking for him,
and my sister, haggard, sloshed,
offers me a miniature infant
in the palm of her hand, flicks
a remark, nonchalant, jokey,
about my lack of sons.
I think of crunching
the newborn in my fist.

I am looking for him, as if
protection were possible, as if
rescue required only
that I lay eyes on him,
explain a few things —
what makes a sand dollar,
why the ocean has salt.

Carol V. Davis

ON A SUBURBAN STREET

The snake lay across the threshold
pretending it was nothing but a snake.
The rest of that day the hours broke
off in chunks, scattering into the scrub,
drifting back as the light shifted.
Next morning a spider crawled
from the stainless steel drain.
One pair of legs raised like scepters.
He declared the kitchen his,
dared me to turn on the faucet.
Then the crows returned.
A Greek chorus, black-hooded on the front lawn.
No scolding caws, just the pierce of accusation.
Nothing had changed.
And yet a divide between silence and noise.
In the backyard squirrels scampered up
the orange tree, burned-out lanterns
of hollowed fruit in their wake.
The mockingbirds and warblers taunted,
bluebirds shrieked.
Along the street violet-tinged feathers wove
into a fence, rising and falling in the breeze.
Guarding the house from the evil eye
or a warning sign to others?
The sidewalk heaved from tree roots,
its lip split from an earthquake.
At dusk machine gun rumble: *caw-caw-caw.*
The heads of the crows bobbing as they reload.

PRESENCE

Kay Ryan

PAIRED THINGS

Who, who had only seen wings,
could extrapolate the
skinny sticks of things
birds use for land,
the backward way they bend,
the silly way they stand?
And who, only studying
birdtracks in the sand,
could think those little forks
had decamped on the wind?
So many paired things seem odd.
Who ever would have dreamed
the broad winged raven of despair
would quit the air and go
bandylegged upon the ground,
a common crow?

Peg Quinn

THE CROW'S CALLING

A bird moved as if
a black hole shaped
like a crow was strutting
a path across bright playground
grass before rising, leisurely,
at an angle, to observe
from the perch
of a stark eucalyptus

to caw forth a sermon,
determined, inspired as a priest
on a foreign mission

ignoring the fact of our
language difference.

Melinda Palacio

DISCONCERTED CROW

if only his bird suit fit, he
grumbles and caws, drives
away his dove friends, he
pecks at uneven bristles, he
flaps and folds starched wings.
familiar feathers hang all wrong
like borrowed funeral clothes

far from dead, he
disrobes with a thud,
lands on my roof, he
morphs into a toddler,
crashes giant steps, he
skates swift on loose shingles
calls out to his pity of doves

when no one answers, he
takes up his post on a wire
outside my window, he
hunches his seaweed back,
beak snug in breast, and he
is an old man again

Ann Stanford

THE COMMITTEE

Black and serious, they are dropping down one by one to the top
      of the walnut tree.
It is spring and the bare branches are right for a conversation.
The sap has not risen yet, but those branches will always be bare
Up there, crooked with ebbed life lost now, like a legal argument.
They shift a bit as they settle into place.
Once in a while one says something, but the answer is always the same,
The question is too — it is all *caw* and *caw*.
Do they think they are hidden by the green leaves partway up the branches?
Do they like it up there cocking their heads in the fresh morning?
One by one they fly off as if to other appointments.
Whatever they did, it must be done all over again.

devorah major

SAN FRANCISCO CROWS

when i was a child
there were no crows
in san francisco

no wild crows
sleek, black and full
of harsh, assaulting song

no crows
fat and raucous
settling on tree branches
perched on house eaves
squatting on cable wires.

there were pigeons
with their incessant coos
and sheets of white waste
coating sidewalks and roofs

and there were many
worm-glutted robin redbreasts
and the gifts of hummingbirds
who hovered above fragrant
jasmine blossoms

and sweet, chirping sparrows
bringing in the dawn
and red-tailed hawks
circling high before the dive
to capture squirrel or rat

and, of course
swooping down on leftovers
of schoolyard lunches

but there were no crows
like there are now, now
so many crows
filling our streets
with dark discord

heavy, somber omens
in the shadows they cast.

Sheila Golburgh Johnson

AFTER THE FIRE

It was quiet. The brush-covered hills
that used to thrill the air with birdsong,
silent. The few leaves left on the burned trees
were pale brown bats hanging upside down.

One day I heard a guttural *Caaaw,*
       Caaaw, and in a tangle of roots
jutting from the hillside I spotted a crow,
preening in the haze, turning its beak
from side to side as if to sniff
the smoke-scented air.

The next morning there were three.

Later the burned ground filled with crows
cawing and stalking, each in a brash walk,
swinging its shoulders with every bowlegged step,
scooping up lizards and bugs without breaking stride.

Weeks later a scrub jay, that raucous
nuisance of the canyon, showed up,
welcome this time. Its blue back was
a cool flash of color among the black
crows, black earth, black tree trunks.

Other jays came, and one morning
I heard the descending notes of a canyon wren,
the fruity song of a white-crowned sparrow.
Months passed, and finally one dawn rang
with the cooing of mourning doves, the chirping
of finches, the clicking and murmuring of a quail
family parading in line, crests bobbing and
their watch-quail perched nearby, ready to sound an alarm.

Not a crow in sight.

June Sylvester Saraceno

THIS WINTER

The crows seem larger than life.
That one there — big as a cow,
sheen of jet feathers, marble-eyed surveyor,
gauges me as I approach.

Maybe it is a shift in proportion
brought on by winter.
My shadow wanes, dulled grey
and somewhat featureless on the frost.
The crow is an inky country by contrast.

This indifferent crow holds his ground.
I consider running madly at him,
flapping to startle him into flight.
Then I consider the ditch between us
and continue my slow pace.

Passing, I see something dangles
from his beak — entrails? A dark ribbon?
The shoelace of the last person
who tried to jar him into the sky?

"You win," I mutter under my breath.
A little uneasy at his presence behind me,
outside of my vision, I speed up slightly,
as though moving towards a deadline
that must be met.

Robert W. Evans

BOREL HILL

Over Borel Hill, I saw a ragged crow
flying backward. He didn't want to,
but the great, cold rush of north wind
that hadn't slowed since Alaska
was stronger than his wings.
He rowed that air like a hero,
but he was losing ground.

Then he seemed to recall an ancient,
avian strategy, and, folding his wings,
he fell straight down like a sleek,
black missile, a kamikaze dive,
but just before he hit
he pulled out and swooped forward,
gaining ground to slip in behind
the wind shadow of the hill.

There are times I wish I had
an ancient strategy, a charmed
amulet, or magician's trick
that I could use to anchor myself,
maybe gain some ground
on that invisible flow
that's holding me back.

Or I'd settle for a way to use this knowledge
that's come so hard, these nuggets
of truth I've dug out of the mistakes
and failures of my life — like turnips
hacked from November earth — for example,
the unexpected sense that sometimes
you have to give up, stop fighting,
and just fall in the right direction.

LIKENESS

Jeanette Clough

INTO THE FOURTH GATE:
DIALOGUE WITH BIRDS

The fourth gate is always open. Birds fly through it, over, and around. Occasionally a mink or fox arrives, and the hunger of all predators disappears. The gate makes no judgment.

A curtain of parrots fills the fourth gate. The din is tremendous. A sparrow hawk flies through and the parrots scatter. I say to a raven, "Some birds and humans kill their own kind." The raven replies, "Fragile crackling in the nest."

The fourth gate is in a field, a marsh, a wood, desert, or tundra. The birds have no need to be elsewhere. They are restless nevertheless, coming and going at their own pace. To leave the fourth gate, ducks may walk a dozen steps but migrating geese will fly for days. Eight flamingos land in the shallows.

Nothing stays long at the fourth gate. Landscape, birds and weather rearrange in a blink. I say to a woodpecker, "You hammer at the gate but build no nest." The woodpecker replies, "Wing, and stir the air." The woodpecker flies away.

A breeze sighs through the gate and the gate disappears. I say to the raven, "Here the singing of telephone wires is clearer than the singing of birds." The raven replies, "Exactly and balanced on a thin bright line."

Mary Rudge

CROW, EVERYTHING YOU SAY

Crow, I am bilingual now so know
everything you say, as you look through windows,
from trees, at unmade beds, tossed sheets,
as you compare our naked bodies with the
people's down the street.
My obsession is the writing down —
your croaking talk about how, three blocks over,
shiny things you like are in the room
(hoping a window opens and you can steal).
                                    You tell
where you find eclectic things to eat,
how old-neon the city's heart is, still,
and how you love the babies that you hatched,
taking another's nest, another's eggs —
different species, different color? — Still birds.
                                    I heard
a random bullet brought your buddy down.
You left a memorial of twigs and pebbles on
the sidewalk where his body fell — quite a few
of you, tears rolled down your beaks.
I hear the heartbreak crack in your caw
                        as you speak.
                                    You let me know
no crows hobo as before, no one flies north and
south for seasons or seeks forest sanctuary;
you are a tough town-gang, changed from —
sure, there's more — qualities of air and light?
I'm writing that down, too, will soon
know all I need about a former wildness,
elements, the power of flight,
a closeness to the stratosphere of God —
you once flew and remember
wind on wings, and thunder.

Crow, I know your language now,
and you're talking my poems.

Kim Shuck

THE COMMITTEE

Those black birds they've
Taken to perching on the fence when I'm
Out in the garden just
Companionable sometimes scratching
Raven odes or research notes into the
Pressure treated wood they
Were known for guarding things
Watching for things holding the
Evil down this
Group will
Wrestle my neighbor for a pizza box on
Trash night but me they
Just watch, follow as I weed I
Sometimes wonder if I'm a shiny thing or a
Transgression
Wonder what they've caught me at

Philip Levine

THE THREE CROWS

At dawn my great aunt Tsipie would rise and go
to the east windows of the apartment,
face the weak October sun and curse God.
A deeply spiritual woman, she could roll
strudel dough so fine even the blind could see through it.
Overweight, 62, worn out
from mothering three daughters and one husband
— an upholsterer on nights at Dodge Main —
she no longer walked on water or raised
the recently dead. Instead she convened
at noon from her seventh story back porch
with heaven's emissaries, three black crows
perched in the top branches of the neighborhood's
one remaining oak. Stuffed with strudel,
safely inside the screen door, I heard
her speak out in Ukrainian Yiddish
addressing the three angels by their names.
They would flutter their greasy, savage wings
in warning and settle back. "Fuck with me,"
they seemed to say, "You fuck with Him on high."
The hardness of eyes, the sureness of claws,
the incessant caw-cawing of their voices,
the incandescence of feathered wings,
of gleaming beaks, all this she faced down.
Who brought the sharp wheeze to her grandson's chest?
Who left her youngest simple? Who put Jake,
her husband, crooked back and all, on nights?
For minutes on end the three crows listened
and gave nothing in return. I could say
to all those who live in God's green kingdom,
her grandson grew into a tall young man,
Jake made it to days, simple Annie,

her daughter, learned to sew by hand at last,
for in truth all this happened. Even Yenkel,
her dearest brother, given up for lost
thirty years before, escaped from prison
in the pine forest of Siberia
to make his way to Michigan. Can you hear
the ax buried in a foreign tree, the child
floating like ashes above the lost town,
can you hear the vanished world? I remember
the three crows, especially their silences.
I remember Tsipie's voice, high and sweet,
going out on her breath of milk and tea,
asking to be heard. When the crows took off,
I remember the high branches quivering
before the world stilled. The three birds rose
imperiously above the roof tops
until they disappeared into a sky
long ago gone gray above our lives,
only to plummet surely back to earth.

David Oliveira

Excerpt from
MAP OF THE KNOWN WORLD

It is when walking here among the tall scrub,
my feet stepping into clay ruts carved
by someone's lost tires during last season's last rain,
that I think to ask this simple question:
How many times have I looked up without noticing the sky?
Even now, if not for the sudden appearance of the crow,
I would probably be thinking about food.
This seems to be my life's work,
though, if you ask me for the record,
I would say I was about my father's business,
building a philosophical frame
on which to hang the advancement of the race.
Everyone knows a race travels on its stomach,
and thus I am forgiven — at least, by myself — and by the crow,
whose only thought uncannily mirrors my own.

Halie Rosenberg

THE COMPANY OF CROWS

When my mother was left alone
In our house by the lake
She took to feeding the birds

Hoping for blue jays and finches
All she got were the rowdy crows
Loud and squawking, they demanded
Breakfast every morning

She liked feeling needed
And began buying rye
She said it was their favorite

They would swoop and dive-bomb the deck
Screaming and fighting for the crusts
They would perch in the weeping willows and devour

But one often stayed
Perched on the railing, cocking his head
Peering at her through the glass

She named him Sam
He had a broken beak
I think she liked his imperfection
Maybe he was just easy to identify

He would bring her red pieces of twine
A shiny bottle cap
A rubber band

She said they were thank-you gifts
A regal gentleman
Apologizing for unruly friends

She would talk through the window
Save him the butt of the bread
The best piece

None of the other crows fought for it
It was like they knew
Sam was their connection

When the snow came
Her cockeyed friend went missing
The others noticed too
Screams echoed off the frozen lake

My mother didn't know what to do
She cleared ice off the rail
Left more bread than usual

But the food was taken away
By beaks that weren't cracked
Creatures who didn't say thanks

It wasn't the same

And my mother said she cried
When she was left alone again
In our house by the lake

Enid Osborn

I Knew Two Crows

He suffered me to pick him up
and carry him home,
this young, broken bird
who'd fallen into our well.

Later, he took food from my hand;
there was no other way to eat.
I chased away the mockingbirds
who swooped down, crying *Murderer!*

He cocked his head when I spoke,
squawked when I came home,
followed me about the yard
with his shining black eye.

I was not a girl who talked to dolls,
not a lonely girl, but alone.
He was the friend I chose for myself.
He was my crow.

His sister had the very same accident, fell
into the well under the nesting tree, but we
got to her before she flailed against the rocks.
She was waterlogged, but not broken.

We took her home and lodged her
with her brother. He retired to his corner.
In the night, she got on top of him and
pecked him to death. Then she ate his eye.

I looked until the scene went flat,
and still knew not what to make of it.

When I lifted him, mites ran to my hand.
I screamed and dropped his sack of feathers.

My mother knew something about birds.
She said her chickens would do the same
to the weakest chicken.

I knew two crows. One was stronger.
What more was there to know?

Roe Estep

OF CROWS AND THINGS

You say the crow sits
in the same spot each day
while you turn the soil
plant your favorite flower seeds
He gets close to watch
your hands move through the earth
his head tilts as if he knows
the order of things
He talks in squawks
the sound is comforting since
dad left for another town
another life
There's a familiarity
between you and the crow
both in need of company
both in a known routine
He stays close to you for years
perches just above the eave
sometimes hops down
to stand on the old wagon
at the edge of the garden
You pour your heart out
he listens with great intensity
often he answers

We lose you
in late fall
winds chill to the bone
The crow is just outside the window
on a branch of the old oak
He listens and waits
moves back and forth
tries to see you

hear your voice
the one that leaves him tethered
to here and now
There is no sound to resonate
no sound to move his heart
so he sits lifeless
rides the wind
that moves the oak

On a Sunday
we bury you
in a valley just a ways
from the house
The crow
follows the procession
circles above
comes to rest on the limb
of a sapling

The preacher speaks
his words echo
Then the crow speaks
a soft caw, then louder
We turn toward the tree
He speaks one last time
to his friend at rest
his eulogy low and deep
I wonder what he thinks
how he grieves absence
as he stands
solemn and still
like the starkness
of this day
where his voice
trails the wind
to that place
of souls

Ellaraine Lockie

ENCOUNTERS WITH CROWS

The *caw-caw* from low in the acacia tree
grated like sandpaper
Too close and aggressive to be conversational
More like the threat of thunder
Or an adrenaline needle plunged into memory
of a black storm a foot from my face
Eyes as still as the storm's center
offset by slap of wings and flap of beak

The cause of a daily walk with weapons
An umbrella or baseball bat
and the armor of a wide-brimmed hat
Yet the pummeling from my own heart
The rock of dread so heavy and deep that Hitchcock
has buried his playground scene beneath it

These ghosts do not rest in peace
They peck away wanting recognition
for the job of nature's clean-up crew
For transforming death into life
They want awareness of black bigotry
and encroachment on orchards and fields
By those who hear the unnerving calls but not
the varied clicks, rattles and bell-like tones
Music ignored by those
who mistake the need for nest hair
as an act of aggression

One morning the sky blurs with half notes
Airwaves carry a cacophony of caws
In the oak tree hundreds of crows
hunch their shoulders with each cry
A sandpaper shield covers a baby fallen from its nest

And I feel the rock move in my chest
The *whoosh* of wings as Hitchcock's ghosts fly away

Handfuls of cat food litter the patio now
A plastic bag with brown curly hair protruding
from holes hangs from an oak tree
I sometimes sit in the backyard straining to hear
sounds that hint of childhood church bells
Like it was Easter Sunday

David Starkey

ST. FRANCIS DISROBES

Angels come to him at Mass,
whisper of a Kingdom where
everyone's been stripped
of everything unnecessary.

He gazes out the window.
Only a moment ago, every creature
contested with its fellow
for a share of the spoils.

But now, he steps out
into Assisi's public square.
Off come his shoes, his cloak,
his tunic and his hose.
He tosses his staff
onto the paving stones.

Let them all think he's daft —
the sun and breeze feel wonderful
on his bare skin, and already the ravens
are flocking to his outstretched arms.

JOKER

Paul Fericano

CURLY HOWARD MISREADS EDGAR ALLAN POE

The director yells *Cut!* and everyone on the set
is relieved to feel the weight of the day lifted
like a dark comedy of unscripted errors,
no one more thankful than Curly Howard
who retreats to his trailer for a quick smoke and a drink,
rubbing as he goes his shaved cue ball head
where once the hair grew so thick
he actually appeared handsome to women
who fought to run their fingers through it.

He's reminded now of the sacrifices he's made,
the punishment he endures at the onscreen hands
of his older brother, Moe, who lovingly calls him Babe,
the mixed emotions he feels with each conk on the head,
each slap of the face or fingers poked in bewildered eyes,
and all the bricks and bottles and picks and shovels
and falling pianos and entire buildings collapsing
down around him in heaps of lowbrow humor and pain
can't hide the desperation of his clownish art,
the dreary midnight in his laughter.

Sitting alone, the alcohol convinces him otherwise
and he imagines himself a student of serious literature,
finding wisdom in the works of Edgar Allan Poe,
reading tales of unspeakable horrors befalling others,
grateful for this small refuge of scholarly insight,
and he commits to memory poems of young love dying,
mourning loss in a small room, much like this one,
childlike and powerless to rescue the slipping away,
the black doom of wings waiting above the door,
and he reads as he rocks, repeats the line
Quoth the raven, 'Nevermoe,' over and over again,
until he knows it to be absolutely true.

John F. Buckley and Martin Ott

THIRTEEN WAYS OF LOOKING BY A BLACK BIRD

I.
Two murders live in the Financial District on either side of Market
Street. My clan owns the north and west, directions of finality
and wisdom. The others are silly lords of south and east, sunblind
with rising optimism, sighing of migrations they will never take.

II.
There's no time for crying in this pigeon-pecking municipality
with egg-white omelettes wafting from Mission meth houses.
Punks, stare into our inky eyes and tattoo us on wormy necks!
Peer into the shadows after your warehouse rave, and despair.

III.
Candlestick Park sucks as a battlefield. The loyal minions of Odin
and Morrigan suffer through endless pitches, swings, spurts
and delays without one good skirmish leaving steaming meat on
misty ground. We prefer Hunters Point for our favorite pastime.

IV.
We like to scare the tourists on the wharf by snapping up bread
and spitting it back onto the docks like gooey baby-doll heads.
The bison in Golden Gate Park are convinced that we will one day
trample the fence and stampede steak munchers. Oh, the carnage!

V.
Semi-suburban living-room window. My reflection superimposed
over Heckle and Jeckle on the flat television screen. A hound dog
ululating in comic consternation at the magpies' machinations.
Outside, I sit in a fir and decline Latin nouns, eyeing my doubles.

VI.
We have bullied the parrots of Telegraph Hill to steal for us,
posing with tourists atop the crookedest street in the world. Wallets

and iPods are smuggled by bat to Russian Hill, where we jam out
to Black Eyed Peas atop settler bones in eucalyptus money nests.

VII.
Out in the Richmond, we hide up high in the fog and mock a man
who claims to run a laundromat, imitating his Soviet-prison curses
in raspy tones as we bombard the heated leather seats of his new
convertible with pebbles, headless mice and escorts' business cards.

VIII.
Spooky, a one-winged raven, swears that Coit Tower is a doomsday
rocket designed to send an elite gaggle of their airborne commandos
to a future ruled by apes and seagulls. There they will learn to fish
with lasers and blow all mammals back to the Stone Age. Ravens rule!

IX.
When we soar into the clouds, San Francisco is shaped like the perfect
dung ball, the legendary bowel creation from Lord Crowlin who made
the land and man from his fertile tail feathers. We prepare for the end
of days by checking each new poo for signs of the second coming.

X.
I spy with my sharp black eyes a discarded bag of limp French fries.
In the dreamworld, they are bait for catching human toddlers, my
beak delving above their fatty cheeks for round wet morsels, into
their mouths to snatch tongues: immédiatement, je parle français.

XI.
I found them, the berries, the shiny red berries, I found the shiny
red fermented red berries that are red and I ate them up. Now I
feel odd and can't fly. I lie on the ground under the bush and look
at my feet. They have twiggy toes and are funny. Hello, my feet!

XII.

I have memorized the dark paths, the scarred paths on the backlip
of my eyelids as I slumber, fearing fire, poison. I dream about being
inside scarecrows, and legions of men spasming from pies with wings.
I yearn to turn talons into fingers and sew buckshot from barrel eyes.

XIII.

Brylcreem on the ebony plumage for maximum gloss, we emanate cool,
a magical avian slickness. Toss the nestlings spare bugs, pocket change,
diadems of snail entrails, and watch them chase squirrels onto cable tracks.
The shadows hold us between worlds, and we adore the shivering masses.

Jim Natal

LOST: ONE-FOOTED ADULT CROW. REWARD.

Maybe the sign should have said: "FREE"
instead of "LOST." Maybe it's the same crow I hear
down the block puncturing the morning with insistent
counterpoint to the soap-smooth Sunday dove songs.
And "LOST" to whom? One creature's lost
is another's escape. But now that it's back
among the power lines and madronas, this crow
really could be adrift, homeless and dressed
in shabby black, roosting in doorways
wrapped in atrophied wings.

There's the obvious question of how the crow lost
its foot, what led to its pet name of Hopalong, Gimpy,
or, perhaps, Lefty. Did it happen when it was young or grown?
Or was it born that way, its whole life a balancing act?
Crows are so smart. Curiosity or boredom
could have gotten the better of it. And with sharp-edged
suddenness, the idea of spending its maturity in someone's care
became more necessary than ludicrous: kind words,
a guaranteed ear, the certainty of scheduled meals,
a place to sleep with both eyes closed.

And about that reward: If the crow is returned,
accepts again its cage and perch or even comes back
on its own to reclaim its low-ceilinged kingdom,
will it be win-win all around? The owner regains
a live-in jester. The crow can relax, take a load off its foot.
And the alert-hearted Samaritan, who at first
refused the crisp twenty, now slips it in
with the other bills on the way down the back stairs.
It's almost like one of those Asian teaching tales —
how the unfortunate open window leads in as well as out.

Andre Levi

HERMES PLAYS POKER WITH RAVEN

I sat down with the trickster gods and heroes
to play a game of poker, and we all five-card studs.
Full of guile, I convinced them
to let me deal them out the hands.
Raven, stealer of daylight, suspected me from the first,
for I spun with my sinister left hand
and gave them mismatched jokers, trumped I well.
I gave myself both airs and aces wild.
His beady eyes fixed on me, darkness fell,
my hand faltered for a moment,
and then I gave that corbie one brave jack.
Krishna dawdled, playing his wind-flute
like a panpipe, an old harmonica,
"I'm Too Blue for You."
His azure skin glowed green by firelight.
Coyote howled and changed his shape
to a baleful, wizened gambler, a card shark
with giant teeth and lust for blood.
But I had myself been a shape-shifter,
a young man, an old man,
a girl, a guide,
a psychopomp to Hades' land,
and had no fear. The winner of all
would get to kiss the spinning hands
of one Fate, Atropos. I loved her from afar.
But I had not counted on Loki, son of giants,
destroyer of the best-laid plans
of messengers of gods.
He had returned victorious
from his long prison of torment,
switched all the rules, and made ten aces rise.
He won the game and paid the gods of chaos cash,
though Raven bit his hand off in the dark.

W. K. Gourley

CROW ADVISES CLAUDE, THE BIRD HUNTER

Miracles occur,
If you care to call those spasmodic
Tricks of radiance miracles.

— Sylvia Plath, "Black Rook in Rainy Weather," 1956

Claude, you have a faulty view of my kin.
Our *Corvus* family is not responsible
for foot-tracks around your eyes
or measuring a straight flying distance.
We would not stoop to metaphor
abasement, such as "eating human."

We have no coffined cemeteries,
but listen to our wail sounding above
your locked and unrecycled bodies.
We have no plans for global
thermonuclear war
or *Arbeit Macht Frei* camps.
We train no boy soldiers
and hold no girl slaves.
Our females don't dance
unfeathered on poles
We give our young nests
and wings.

Yes, Claude,
watch for our feather-sheen,
our eye-shine, and the flash
of our moments of consequence.
Pay attention to our blacktalk
and hear the beauty of your Maria Callas
in our pellucid morning trill,
Caw   Caw   Caw-Caw-Caw.

Hunter, emerge from your blind.
See miracle in us.

Barry Spacks

THE STROLLING CROW
— for Bob Brill

Clumping along down the college path
like a proper man on a morning stroll
comes a cocky crow, as wide a crow
and tall and sleek and true a crow
as you'd ever see.

As nice a crow as I'll ever be.

I didn't expect to meet a crow
in just that way.
Pompous crow: pushy crow:
sharp and fat as a muscle-flex.
Left-step out, peck-glance, step right:
humorous crow: neighborly crow:
focus of light. Disinterested light.

But goodness knows, the cause of the crow's
strange strolling here
is clear as clear:

A crow can't hover
in the empty air
forever.

2.
Crows on the highway, nailing down
a sometime rabbit.

Crows on the housetops. Crows on the lawn.
Beaks rivet.

Kin to vulture, raven, kite.
But crows are gayer.

This strolling crow, he passes like
an overseer.

Who'd expect a crow so wise
he'd nod? Implausible.

Come strolling crow, crow civilized,
anything's possible!

3.
I'll take a crow for my emblem beast
in the game we play, "Reveal Your Soul,"
at faculty parties. Even though
the Grand Massif, moustached and piped,
who teaches history — man you'd think
would act the lion — speaks Gazelle,
few'd choose a crow. Not even though
our loveliest lady's known to pick
pike in the lake, and once a snake
— she was tired that night, she was feeling like a saint,
she was dreaming of the sun on her saurian back —

but a *crow*?

4.

That's me, that's me, purebred crow,
black as a splinter of anthracite coal,
bumpy old umbrella in a fumbly wind,
hard without if soft within,
sure and clean as a painted skull
and shiny as a pocket comb:
bothered by a stuffed shirt:
awkward as a torn sheet
flopping on the laundry line —
rinsowhite turned inside out —

an honest creature:
rapacious in my nature:
formal dress: an agile eye:
clumping down the college path,
glancing right, glancing left:
what bird he'd be may mean the life
or the death of a man. Old crow,
pass on!

Friday Lubina

BLACKEST BIRD OBSESSION

your lustrous darkness
lurches about my lawn
like a porn store shopping
bag in a breeze
       only calculated

your movements are determined
and purposeful
you gallop from commuters and garbage men
       and back to center road
to investigate a reflective object
like a child crippled with A.D.D.

your cries comfort and arouse me
my senses pricked by the flash
of a hunkered-down shadow against
the warmly lit morning wall
followed by a throaty vibration, almost
belching from atop the light pole
outside my office window

i sit still
with murderous yearning
wishing myself small, perched under sable wings
grooming plumes, keeping your flight
both comfortable and efficient

Perie Longo

CROWS' FEET

It is no fun to wake up and find yourself
the oldest person in the group, probably
the only one who counts how many crows
have come to tramp around the eyes
looking for some code to crack.
"Haven't you had enough of me?" I grump,
but they're greedy, these crows,
now they want *under* my eyes. They remind me
their mark is poetic, those lines indication
of frequent flights, squints,
journeys to far ranges and slim passes.
I ask them to walk where they're not apparent,
behind my knees, for instance,
I don't leave my grubby hand prints all over
their sleek wings. It is no fun to wake up
doubting the wisdom required of such sacred marks,
but since I'm told the importance of aging gracefully
I check the mirror for their bad reputation,
consider I'm becoming a little like the earth
and the map they've left
is how the soul finds its way home.

Joan Fallert

EATING CROW & OTHER THOUGHTS

I spoke — and he is not
speaking.

Because I dared
he is Not Speaking,
a trick Adam picked up the moment
he found himself outside the Garden,
as if expulsion were not enough.

All song and sound is damped now.
Even profound silence is something
I cannot hear; only the heart's sore impulse
reaches my ear.

I saw Madness last night
and almost took her hand when
she beckoned like some old tragic ghost;
yet I could not follow,
stopped in my own tracks
by his quicksand mind.

Wasn't it Miriam who questioned whether God spoke
only through Moses, and was stricken
with leprosy for not holding her tongue?
But God is good and she was
cured as soon as she recanted and apologized.

From this angle, crow fills
the whole window.

Rude, despised bird — how often I have been made
to eat you.
Still, I can't help liking your big, bold blue-blackness,
your certain eye,
the thwat-whack you make on the roof
and — when you fly —

Cathryn Andresen

PASS THE SALT

feathers and shine   ebony
fluff   those scrawny bones seem
barely enough on

which to gnaw to balance
an error   innocent or
not   in need of repair   loss

of face a humbling
fate   crow du jour is
a weighty plate

Cynthia Anderson

A PARABLE

The ravens saw garbage
and knew that it was good.
They saw roadkill — even better.
They became fruitful and multiplied,
an explosion made possible
by humans, who struck back
with bullets and poison. No luck.
Like capitalists run amok,
ravens show up uninvited,
squawking and diving,
looking for coyotes to torment
and tortoises for dessert.
Too much like us for comfort,
they kiss, commit adultery, even speak.
One learned to say, *Bad Edgar. Nevermore.*
Another mimicked a detonation team —
Three, two, one, *Kaboom!*
The only way to tame ravens
would be to blow up the world.
They're chained to us, thriving
on our worst — dark reminders
of the sprawl of our desires.

Dian Sousa

INTO THAT DARKNESS PEERING

Deep into that darkness peering,
long I stood there wondering, fearing...
— Edgar Allan Poe, "The Raven"

One large black wing has wedged itself through a crack in the street.
It is sticking up like a feathery dorsal fin stuck in a cement current.
My neighbors and I have gathered around it.
Sam pokes it with a stick. Bruce wants to get a crowbar,
pry open the road and reveal the mystery.
When he says this out loud, ravens start to gather in a circle around us.
It is probably just coincidence, but no one wants to speculate.
Suddenly no one wants to say anything.
The circle of ravens is six rings deep and growing.
It is starting to look like a moat filled with shiny ink
and sharp beaks, and we're the crumbling human castle.

The circle of ravens is tightening. Sam is white-knuckling his stick,
silently begging it to become a machine gun.
Bruce is wishing he had the crowbar.
I'm wondering why we can't just shoo them away.
We know we are bigger, but somehow our heavy bones
and meaty legs seem slow and wrong now.
Sam's turquoise polo shirt and Bruce's Red Sox cap
start to look like the grotesque appendages
of prehistoric animals we've never heard of
because they couldn't blend in with the trees or the rocks
or the shifting light of a forest floor,
and therefore were eaten so quickly
even their tiniest, fragmented shadow became a lost hallucination.
Even in their obsolescence, those weird animals
probably believed they were too beautiful to have to adapt.
The pavement is collapsing.
A large black wing is starting to rise.

Messenger

Julianna McCarthy

JANUARY

When snow brings sleep and silence covers all,
Raven dreams skyward to pluck the light once more
from heaven's roof. Waking, framed funereal
against the ash-gray sky, brown fields before
him capped in spinning white, the wind roars
echo to his hoarse quork and rattle call —
to hunt with corvid cunning, swooping low
for any darting, glint-eyed catch — he alone
champion, prime, primal, predatory one
can hold back cold, hunger, death and night.
Norse god Hrafn, who first captured the sun,
hurled it down to make the dark world bright,
black against the crystal curtain soaring
pine high, greets winter's stroke upon his wing.

Danusha Laméris

THE CROWS RETURN

No nightingales are these,
the hundred or so graceless travelers
who swarm and caw,
thicken the peach blossom sky,
then land on the thin, black wires.

Below, the oily gutters,
cars lined up along an endless
stretch of asphalt,
the last light glinting off their fenders.

What urgency
has brought them here,
this murder of messengers,
cacophony of barbed voices?

Maybe they're the Dead
returned, come to tell us
they're not elsewhere, but here,
between the low cloud layer
and rotting loam.

That while we mourn for them,
all along they have been
calling back to us
in their loudest, harshest songs.

Patricia Wellingham-Jones

A RAVEN RIDES HIS SHOULDER

He pushes his tired body
behind the wheel of his '89 Chevy truck,
drives to his second full-time
job of the day.

Last week
his 83-year-old mother died.

Guilt digs in its claws
like a raven riding his shoulder.
He okays the $600 in flowers that smell
decayed before the funeral begins.

Lets his dad choose the mahogany
casket with pink silk lining, solid brass handles.
He loads corpse and coffin
into his pickup, crawls behind the wheel again.

Leading a caravan to the coast,
he crams the family into motel rooms,
pays the undertaker, tips hirelings,
passes out tissues, swallows his tears.

He wonders if he can push his body
through one more job.
Driving home through rain-shrouded mountains,
he watches dark birds lift from drooping boughs.

Jennifer Arin

FORCE OF NATURE

Certain forms of nature — dogs, ravens, crows —
recognize weakness and instinctively close
in on the injured; today, as the ocean's
spray turns its sand to sludge, the meager motions

of a sandpiper stuck in that grainy mud
stir my curiosity, and the blood
of carnivorous birds that blackly stretch
their claws toward the wounded, and swoop, and etch

into my mind the hard way nature feeds.
With an unsplit stick found when a wave recedes,
I wave away the predators, who soon know
my fight or flight instinct as I land a blow

on a pitbull's skull, since its owner chooses
not to call it off the bird; instead he muses
aloud how nature preys upon itself when ill:
"If the dog doesn't get it, crows and ravens will."

Worse, an angry swell the ocean sends to shore
submerges the bird, pulls it toward that cold floor.
Chasing the sea, I spot that hurt, familiar wing,
catch the bird with both hands, and foolishly sing

while carrying it, beat by heartbeat, to the car,
then to a vet who brusquely says the wing's far
gone, he'll put the bird to sleep — oh, but I
didn't come this far to help a living thing die!

Mad as the new rain, I try a desperate last plan;
the aviary, refuge from all predators, can —
and will — care for this fragile life.
Witness: it survived nature's ready knife.

Deborah A. Miranda

MY CROW

I know I will travel to heaven in the guts of a crow —
each of us assigned transportation at birth, marked

upon our arrival in smoggy cities, cold mountains, green lakes,
deserted parking lots. That's why God made so many crows, you see:

no body forgotten, no flesh left undigested. A time to live,
a time to die, a time to re-enter Creation through

the lift of blackest feathers. I can pick my crow out
of a crowd despite identical sleek pinions

and clacking black beaks — he's something special, not
like the other trash-picking, dirt-talking, rabble-rousing

wannabes, ganging up on juveniles too big for the nest,
too thin for the flock. He stands alone on the bright yellow

centerline, guards fresh possum guts, sticky raccoon entrails,
nicely splattered deer brains; doesn't flinch as I draw closer

in my big steel and plastic boat on wheels. I can't
stare him down; he's just doing his job: recycling

what's too slow, too old, too stupid to live, and I,
I am simply the one he's got his eye on next.

Not today, but thank you, I say as we pass: *Keep up
the good work without me, brother.*

Sojourner Kincaid Rolle

THE PALLBEARERS

— On viewing Van Gogh's "Wheatfield with Crows"

Morning mists move across the vale
A phalanx of birds rises above the golden savannah
Keepers of the road from here to there

It is an ominous thing —

Crows, black shiny eyes keen
Hover above the fields of grain
Cawing at the unseen

The fearful fall — sprawling at the gate
The soul, ready, steps forward
Onto the path

In blinding wisdom
Spirits of the ascended
Bathe the way

Robert Peake

SHELF ROAD, OJAI

The wine-grape eye
dried black and sunken,

black flint blades
of wing feather splayed —

my boyhood self would
roll it with a stick.

The underworld of the body
lies open among the ants.

How can I have become
the grown self now striding past?

The animal body says, *Stop*
to the mind high in flight.

Wind rustles the three of us.

Charan Sue Wollard

KNOWING

She said she would return
as a crow,
swarm on the spiked branches
of Monterey pines
with others of her flock
Not some regal raven,
but a so-so black bird

In life, she dressed
in peacock feathers
and amethyst beads
Now she'll hover,
a dark phantasm

Perhaps in the long days
of her dying
she kenned
an elegant coherence
in the world —
black silhouette
against almond sky

Steve Kowit

RAVEN

Squawks from a raven in what used to be Jack
Funk's field over the fence, scolding
me till I look up & see that the hills
are still there, that the day
couldn't be lovelier, sweeter. Susan Green's
little girls are chatting in singsong
up in the tree house,
in what used to be Dempsey's old place
to the west. & who will stroll over these four-
point-five acres of rolling high desert chaparral
when we two are gone? —The tin barn.
The pump house & shed. That underground
stream from which we've been drinking
our fill these dozen years.
Who'll own all this dusty blue mountain lilac,
the aloe & roses & pines & bright orange iceplant?
Who'll walk in the shade of that live oak
under which Ralphie & Ivan & Charlie
& Eddie are buried? Who'll watch the quail
flutter out of the brush & the rabbits
scurry for cover? Who will these granite
boulders & lovely agaves belong to
when you & I, love, are buried
& long forgotten? — Forgive me,
sweet earth, for not being shaken more often
out of the heavy sleep of the self.
Wake up! Wake up! scolds the raven, sailing off
over the canyon. *Wake up! Wake up! Wake up!*

Night-bringer

Cecilia Woloch

LASSWADE, MIDLOTHIAN: DUSK

Crow, I cried, *I need to talk to you.*
The whole sky lurched.
Black wings. Most bitter trees
I've ever seen. Wild daffodils.
Here is a world
that is just as the world was world
before we named it *world.*
Here is a sky that screams back at me
as I rush toward it, darkening.

Joseph Stroud

NIGHT IN DAY

The night never wants to end, to give itself over
to light. So it traps itself in things: obsidian, crows.
Even on summer solstice, the day of light's great
triumph, where fields of sunflowers guzzle in the sun —
we break open the watermelon and spit out
black seeds, bits of night glistening on the grass

Susan Kelly-DeWitt

CROWS AT EVENING

Twilights I see them
      thick as brambles
           of wild grape;

                a black smoke of them, a coil
         of black wires; a royal black
highway paved with feathers.

The light that has been bubbling —
boiling and singing!
in the yellow veins

      of leaves, in the muslin tongues
        of lilies, quiets
           to a muffled

          whisper, a slow
        rose simmer. The treetops
    color like tea stains

against the sky's zodiac
cup, as they pour, a torrent
of oil, as they funnel

       west out of sight;
          a Houdini of crows
          disappearing

      — recalled
   like some genie
into a secret lamp,

into the day's interior
darkness.

Greg Karpain

BECOMING THIS

on the moon-of-the-falling-leaves,
a mooncrow on the top branch
of a sycamore caws out.
I see it is not the crow,
but the tree, calling
out through the crow.
being still, I hear the tree
and the crow, how the crow
speaks for the tree,
like a grandfather
for a child.

in the bright moonlight-of-the-falling-leaves
as the stream wets the roots
of the tree and the mooncrow
only appears as it caws,
the branches knock and rub in the wind,
the wind calling out for them,
like a mother for a newborn.

they make one sound,
leaves of the moon falling
through the breeze, fluttering
between the caws of a crow
and deliberately
to the wet earth
speaking
through the cold stream;

mooncrow, wind, tree, and I,
moon-of-the-falling-leaves,
tangle indistinguishably,
becoming this night,
becoming this.

Lisl Auf der Heide

BLACK BIRDS

When the crows come
black against the darkening sky
their wings obscure the sun
and small sounds drown
in their strident caws.

They storm the walnut trees
snatch the green fruit
drop it from great heights
retrieve the cracked kernels.

Again and again they dive
from tree to ground
feathers gleaming
where stray sunrays touch.

And when the mountains turn blue
with the haze of evening
the crows lift off in ebony formation
head towards some secret roost
where they can blend into night.

Frances Pettey Davis

LAST CROW

Last
crow
of the
evening,
flying dark
as a bat, the
wrong direction,
over the house, not
with the flock (long
passed), errant ebony
splinter cutting sky, we're
tired of your ungainly caw,
shouting over mockingbirds
and sparrow songs. Black
jumpered, audacious
eyed, safe in coal-
dust numbers —
find your own
nation, a tree-
full of your
tarry selves,
and make
it far
from
here.

Connie Post

RAVEN IN FLIGHT

The sky has never forgiven you
for your blackness

when you fly
inside the backdrop of night
I am the only one who sees you

you claw your way
into my dreams
but I cannot
find you in the morning

your beak weighs heavy
on the ruined dusk
I hear your guttural call
when I am running
down to the dry riverbed

I remember the same way
you flew over me
when I was running away
in second grade

how you knew my mother
would find me
how you have pulled
away at the skin
of my regret

years have passed and still
you land at random
on the uneven fence
of silence

always helping me
to understand
what it means to
live as the heretic

to realize
there is no contrition
in the fading light

Kevin Hearle

THE SCARECROW'S SOLILOQUY

Where does the crow go
at night? Everywhere.
Nowhere. The crow is
the night, and the night
is crowing. Listen.

Michael Hannon

WHAT THE CROW SAID

Though friendly to magic
I am not a man disguised as a crow.

I am night eating the sun.

Contributors' Notes

Sylvia Alcon has been a featured reader at the longtime poetry series Corners of the Mouth in San Luis Obispo, and has read in the city's annual poetry festival. Her poems have been published in *Solo Cafe* and in *Poems for Endangered Places*, on which she collaborated with six other poets. For 10 years she's been a member of the Cambria Writers Workshop, where critique and encouragement continue to provide impetus.

Ron Alexander is a psychologist who lives in Santa Barbara with his partner Gary and their calico cats. He wrote poetry in grammar school and college, dropped it for 40 years, then pursued it with renewed passion. His work has recently been published in *Arts & Understanding* and *Askew*, and he is a regular reader at local and regional venues, including the Santa Barbara Poetry Festival.

Maureen Alsop is the author of *Apparition Wren* (Main Street Rag, 2007) and several chapbooks, including *Luminal Equation* (Cannibal Press, 2009) and *the dream and the dream you spoke* (Spire Press, 2009). She is the winner of *Harpur Palate's* Milton Kessler Memorial Prize for Poetry and *The Bitter Oleander's* Frances Locke Memorial Poetry Award. She is an associate poetry editor for *Inlandia: A Literary Journal* and the online journal *Poemeleon*. www.maureenalsop.com

Cynthia Anderson, co-editor of *A Bird Black As the Sun*, lives in the high desert near Joshua Tree National Park. Her poems have appeared in numerous journals and have won awards from the Santa Barbara Arts Council, the Santa Barbara Writers Conference, and the Wildling Art Museum. Her latest book is *In the Mojave* (Pencil Cholla Press, 2011). Her collaborations with her husband, Bill Dahl, are online at www.rainbear.com

Poet and physicist **Len Anderson** is the author of *Affection for the Unknowable* (Hummingbird Press, 2003). His poems have appeared in *Bellowing Ark, DMQ Review, The Montserrat Review, Porter Gulch Review, Quarry West, Red Wheelbarrow, Sand Hill Review, Sarasota Review of Poetry,* and *The Anthology of Monterey Bay Poets 2004*. He is a winner of the Dragonfly Press Poetry Competition and the Mary Lönnberg Smith Poetry Award.

Cathryn Andresen's poetry reflects her interest in relationships between nouns — proper and common. From time to time, her poetry wins an award, appears in print, or is an invited guest at readings. Cathryn edited *Quintessence — An Anthology* (VCWC Press, 2008) and has published her first chapbook, *human / Nature*. She has hosted the Poem-Crafters Guild workshop since its beginnings in 2005. Home is a small ranch in Southern California. She'll tell you, "I live in a garden." www.cathryn-andresen.com

Jennifer Arin's poems and essays have appeared in *The AWP Writers' Chronicle, ZYZZYVA, Poet Lore, The Chronicle of Higher Education, Puerto del Sol, Paris / Atlantic, The San Francisco Chronicle*, and other national and international journals. Her awards include funding from the Spanish Ministry of Culture and grants from the NEA, *Poets & Writers*, and PEN. She teaches in the English department at San Francisco State University.

Rochelle Arellano lives and writes in Gilroy, where she enjoys watching the crows and ravens in and around the hills and open spaces of the beautiful Santa Clara Valley. She says, "I've come to believe ravens and crows know more about us than we do about them; they are keen observers of humans. I like to think we amuse them." Rochelle's poems have been published in *Bathyspheric Review* and *Monterey Poetry Review*.

Born in Vienna, Austria, **Lisl Auf der Heide** came to California at age 16. She has been writing poetry since she was eight. Her poems and stories have appeared in a number of magazines as well as in three poetry collections and several anthologies. She collaborated with her late artist-husband, Ralph Auf der Heide, writing limericks to accompany his paintings.

A native of Copenhagen, Denmark, **Bettina T. Barrett** began writing poems and stories as a teenager in Pennsylvania. She has lived in Santa Barbara since 1972. As an artist, she has widely exhibited her drawings, paintings, and ceramics; as a poet, she has been published in many literary journals; two collections, *Sleepdancer* and *Bear-Star My Name* (Fithian Press, 1994 and 1989); and a chapbook, *HEARTSCAPE* (Mille Grazie Press, 1999).

Abigail (Albrecht) Brandt grew up on the California coast, within earshot of the Pacific Ocean. Her relationship with nature infuses her poems and enhances her life perspective. Her poetry has appeared in numerous journals and anthologies and has received first place state awards in California and Oregon. She currently resides in Salem, Oregon with her beloved husband and collaborator, Werner Brandt. She involves herself with many art forms, including beading, Raku, collage, crochet, and assemblage.

M. L. Brown's poems have appeared in numerous journals, most recently *Blackbird, Eclipse,* and *The Chicago Quarterly Review.* Her manuscript, *Disassembling the Body,* was a finalist in the 2010 Gertrude Press chapbook contest. When not working on her poetry, she devotes her time to fundraising for Planned Parenthood. She has an MFA from Antioch University Los Angeles.

Christopher Buckley teaches creative writing at UC Riverside. He was a Guggenheim Fellow and has received a Fulbright award, four Pushcart Prizes, and two NEA grants. Recent books include *White Shirt* (University of Tampa Press, 2011), *Modern History: Prose Poems 1987-2007* (Tupelo Press, 2008), and *Flying Backbone: The Georgia O'Keeffe Poems* (Blue Light Press, 2008). His book *Rolling the Bones* (University of Tampa Press, 2010) won the Tampa Review Prize for Poetry.

Raised in Michigan but now living in Southern California, **John F. Buckley** and **Martin Ott** began their ongoing games of poetic volleyball in the spring of 2009. Poetry from their collaboration *Poets' Guide to America* has been accepted by more than 30 publications, including *Breakwater Review, Confrontation, Evergreen Review, The Louisiana Review, The Mayo Review,* and *ZYZZYVA*.

Jeanette Clough is the author of three poetry collections: *Island* (Red Hen), *Cantatas*

(Tebot Bach), and *Celestial Burn* (Sacred Beverage). Her poetry has received awards in the Ruskin Competition, the Rilke Competition, Spillway Call and Response Contest, and *Atlanta Review*, and has twice been nominated for a Pushcart Prize. A native of Paterson, New Jersey, she lives in Los Angeles and works as an art researcher.

Constance Crawford began writing as a college student, published a number of short stories in national magazines, and wrote a couple of novels in her thirties and forties. She later published two books of memoir and biography and most recently has turned to poetry with great enjoyment. She lives in Palo Alto.

Patrick Daly's poetry has appeared in Nicholas Kristof's column in *The New York Times* and in the anthology *The Place that Inhabits Us* (Sixteen Rivers Press, 2010). He has received honorable mention in the Pushcart Prizes, and his chapbook, *Playing with Fire,* won the Abby Niebauer Memorial Prize. He and his wife Charlotte Muse co-founded *Out of Our Minds,* a poetry radio show on KKUP in Cupertino. He writes poetry and prose on his lunch hours.

Carol V. Davis won the 2007 T. S. Eliot Prize for *Into the Arms of Pushkin: Poems of St. Petersburg.* Twice a Fulbright scholar in Russia, she was the 2008 poet-in-residence at Olivet College, MI and teaches at Santa Monica College. Her poetry has been read on NPR and Radio Russia. Her new book, *Eating Crow,* is forthcoming in 2012.

Frances Pettey Davis's poems and stories have appeared in *Calyx, The Chattahoochee Review, Vincent Brothers Review, Reed Magazine, Passager, Quercus, Memoir,* and several online poetry journals and anthologies. Her travel writing appears in Avalon Books' *Mexico: A Love Story* (2008) and *Italy: A Love Story* (2006). She received the Lamar York Prize for nonfiction and has been nominated for a Pushcart Prize. She lives in Summerland, where she writes a column for *Coastal View News.*

ellen teaches creative writing at Santa Monica College's Emeritus College. Nominated for Pushcart Prizes in 2008 and 2009, her poems have been published in many venues, including the *Los Angeles Times, Slant, Slipstream, Askew, ACM,* and *Coe Review.* She has won awards from dA Center for Arts in Pomona, *Blue Unicorn,* Cape Cod Times, and others. Her books include *Reverse Kiss* (Main Street Rag, 2005) and *The Gynecic Papers* (Conflux Press, 2005.)

Roe Estep hosted the Ventura Tuesday Night Poetry series for 10 years and an open mic in Santa Paula before that. Her work has been published in local magazines and journals. She says, "I enjoy being outdoors more than anything, with nature and all its offerings. My ideal place is the mountains with serenity and peacefulness, plus a view of the ocean. My interests include clay and woodworking. I find artistic expression is ongoing, and so I keep evolving."

Robert W. Evans has been writing poetry for the last 30 of his 74 years. He was one of the founders of Waverley Writers, a Palo Alto poets group which has been in existence since 1981. In 1994, he received an MFA in creative writing from San Francisco State University. He works full-time as an arborist in the San Francisco mid-peninsula. His other interests include hiking and nature photography.

William Everson (1912-1994), also known as Brother Antoninus, gained renown as a poet during the San Francisco Renaissance. He was a Dominican monk for 18 years, returning to secular life in 1969; between 1971-1981 he was a master letterpress printer at Lime Kiln Press and poet-in-residence at University of California, Santa Cruz. He authored over 20 collections of poetry. "These Are the Ravens" was the title poem of his first book, published in 1935.

Born in New York City, **Joan Fallert,** brought up by a mother who loved and quoted poetry frequently, has had a love affair with language for as long as she can remember. Her poems have appeared in *rivertalk, The Wisconsin Review, Concepts,* and *Shared Sightings,* an anthology of bird poems. She is included in a textbook for gifted high school students and teaches contemporary literature and writing through Santa Barbara Community College's adult education program.

Paul Fericano is a poet, writer, satirist, editor of *The Broadsider,* and co-founder of the first parody news syndicate, *Yossarian Universal News Service.* His work has appeared in *The New York Quarterly, Poetry Now, The Realist, The Wormwood Review, Punch,* and *Krokodil* (Moscow). His poetry books and chapbooks include *The Three Stooges At A Hollywood Party* (24th Street Irregular Press, 2011) and *Commercial Break* (Poor Souls Press, 1982). He divides his time between San Francisco and Santa Barbara. www.yunews.com

Poet, painter, and activist, **Lawrence Ferlinghetti** is the renowned co-founder of City Lights Booksellers & Publishers and author of *A Coney Island of the Mind* (New Directions, 1958), which has sold over a million copies. He has published numerous other volumes of poetry and prose, and has received awards including the National Book Foundation's Literarian Award and the ACLU's Earl Warren Civil Liberties Award. In 2007, he was named Commandeur of the French Order of Arts and Letters.

Nevada City poet **Molly Fisk** is a National Endowment for the Arts fellow and has twice been nominated for Poet Laureate of California. Her two collections are *The More Difficult Beauty* (Hip Pocket Press, 2010) and *Listening to Winter* (Roundhouse Press, 2000). She teaches online at poetrybootcamp.com and helps cancer and cardiac patients boost their immune systems through writing. She's also a radio commentator for NPR and community stations. www.mollyfisk.com

Mary Fitzpatrick is a fourth-generation Angeleno who holds degrees in writing from UC Santa Cruz and UMass Amherst. Her poems have been featured in *Atlanta Review* and *North American Review* as contest finalists, and in several other journals—most recently *Agenda* (UK), *The Dos Passos Review, Askew, Writers at Work.com,* and *The Georgetown Review.* She has three chapbook manuscripts, drives Hwy. 5, and works as an organizational change manager in a large corporation.

Dan Gerber's most recent collection, *A Primer on Parallel Lives* (Copper Canyon Press, 2008) won the Michigan Notable Book Award. His work has appeared in *The Nation,*

The New Yorker, Poetry, The Georgia Review, Narrative, and numerous anthologies. He has published seven other poetry books, three novels, a collection of short stories, and a book on the Indianapolis 500. His work has been selected for *Best American Poetry* and been nominated for two Pushcart Prizes.

W. K. Gourley's poems have appeared in *Tidelines, The Poetry Zone,* and several anthologies. He was a juried poet at the University of Houston Poetry Festival and the recipient of a Downey Scholarship to the Santa Barbara Writers Conference. He is a co-founder of The Fourth Monday Poetry Readers and The Rincon Poets of Santa Barbara. He is a retired professor of surgical pathology.

Lara Gularte was nominated by Bitter Oleander Press for *Best New Poets 2010*. Her work has appeared or is forthcoming in *The Bitter Oleander, Clackamas Literary Review, The Cape Rock, Eclipse, The Evansville Review, The Fourth River, The Haight Ashbury Literary Journal, Hiram Poetry Review, The Montserrat Review, Permafrost, The Sand Hill Review, Watershed, Water-Stone Review,* and *Windfall*. She is an assistant poetry editor for *Narrative* magazine.

Michael Hannon was born in 1939 and began making poems in 1959. He has been widely published in journals and anthologies and is the author of three full-length collections: *Trusting Oblivion* (If Publishing, 2002), *Ordinary Messengers* (Floating Island Publications, 1991), and *Poems and Days* (Isis Press, 1985). Kenneth Rexroth said of his work, "A very good poet indeed, and certainly one of the few Tantric writers in any language who is both profound and witty."

Kevin Hearle is a fifth generation Californian educated at Stanford, Iowa, and UC Santa Cruz. His book *Each Thing We Know Is Changed Because We Know It and Other Poems* (Ahsahta Press, 1994) was a finalist for the National Poetry Series, and his poems have appeared in numerous anthologies, including *California Poetry: From the Gold Rush to the Present* (Heyday Books, 2003).

Katie Goodridge Ingram was born in Mexico to American parents. A chapter from her memoir won the first place award for nonfiction in *New Millennium Writings* 2010, and part of her novel-in-progress received an honorable mention for fiction from New Millennium Writings. She was a co-founder of the Santa Barbara Poetry Festival. Her work has appeared in *A Tribute to Ray Bradbury, Santa Barbara Review,* and *Café Solo,* among others.

Sheila Golburgh Johnson writes nonfiction as well as poetry which has appeared in numerous journals in the U.S. as well as in England, Russia, and Israel. She won the annual Reuben Rose Prize for Poetry offered by *Voices Israel,* and read her poetry at a peace conference in Haifa. Her books are *After I Said No,* an award-winning novel, and *Shared Sightings,* an anthology of bird poetry. She teaches two poetry classes in Santa Barbara.

Greg Karpain received a first place award from the Santa Barbara Poetry Festival and has been published in *rivertalk, Café Solo, Life Times Magazine, Integral Yoga Journal,* and *The Southern Utah Wilderness Association Review*. His chapbooks include *Me and Susie: Poems from the Heart of Chikataw Wash, more like prayers, A Bunch of Crows,* and *Here, Where Everything Is.*

Susan Kelly-DeWitt is the author of *The Fortunate Islands* (Marick Press, 2008), eight small press collections, and three electronic chapbooks. She has been featured on The Writer's Almanac and *Verse Daily,* and her work has appeared in anthologies such as *When She Named Fire: An Anthology of Contemporary Poetry by American Women* (Autumn House Press, 2009) and *Claiming The Spirit Within* (Beacon Press, 1996). www.susankelly-dewitt.com

Kit Kennedy's work has appeared in *Blood Orange Review, California Quarterly, Ginosko, Glass, Pearl, Poems Niederngasse, Rainbow Curve, Runes, Saranac Review,* and *Lavanderia: A Mixed Load of Women, Wash and Word.* With Susan Gangel, she co-authored INCONVENIENCE (Littoral Press, 2010). She hosted the monthly Gallery Café Reading Series in San Francisco from 2006-2010 and blogs at http://poetrybites.blogspot.com

Lois Klein holds a BA in English literature from Tufts University and an MA in psychology from Antioch University. She coordinates the monthly Favorite Poems Project readings in Santa Barbara, is a Fellow of the South Coast Writers Project, teaches through California Poets in the Schools, and leads private writing groups. Her poems have appeared in numerous regional and national journals, and her books include *A Soldier's Daughter* (Turning Point, 2008) and *Naming Water* (Knockinclash Press, 1998).

Steve Kowit has published several collections of his work and a guide to writing poetry, *In the Palm of Your Hand: The Poet's Portable Workshop* (Tilbury House Publishers, 1995). He has received a National Endowment for the Arts fellowship and two Pushcart Prizes. He formerly worked as an animal rights activist and now supports the justice for Palestine movement. He teaches at Southwestern College in Chula Vista and lives on the property described in his poem, "Raven."

Danusha Laméris's work has appeared in *Lyric, Poetry Northwest, Alaska Quarterly Review, The Sun,* and *The Crab Orchard Review,* as well as the anthologies *In a Fine Frenzy: Poets Respond to Shakespeare* (University of Iowa Press, 2005) and *Intimate Kisses* (New World Library, 2003). Her poem "The Interview" was chosen by Naomi Shihab Nye as an honorable mention for *Water~Stone Review's* Jane Kenyon Prize, and she was nominated for Pushcart Prizes in 2009 and 2010.

Noreen Lawlor is a poet and artist who lives in Joshua Tree with her son and two Yorkies. She loves to write about the Mojave Desert and the wondrous creatures who survive there, especially the lone raven who sits atop the Joshua tree surveying her dry domain. She is currently working on a project that combines her graphic art and poems. Several of her poems have been published in *The Sun Runner Magazine* and online.

Andre Levi has a Ph.D. in sociology and teaches in the social sciences. Her poems have appeared in *Sage Trail* and inkbyte.com, among others. Her writing is inspired by her personal and professional interests in social psychology, neuroscience, countercultural arts, and creative processes. When not running, playing music, or saving homeless cats, she can be found writing progressive social commentary, quirky poetry, and even quirkier short stories in Santa Barbara coffeehouses.

Philip Levine, born and raised in Detroit, Michigan, moved to California and taught at California State University Fresno from 1958-1992. He is the author of 16 books of poetry, most recently *News of the World* (Alfred A. Knopf, 2010). His numerous awards include two Guggenheim fellowships, the Ruth Lilly Poetry Prize, the Harriet Monroe Memorial Prize from Poetry, and the Frank O'Hara Prize. In 2011, he was named Poet Laureate of the United States.

Ellaraine Lockie is a widely published poet, nonfiction author, and essayist who has received writing residencies at Centrum in Port Townsend and 11 Pushcart Prize nominations. She has eight chapbooks; the most recent, *Red for the Funeral*, won the 2010 San Gabriel Valley Poetry Festival Chapbook Contest. Her chapbook *Stroking David's Leg* was awarded Best Individual Collection for 2010 by *Purple Patch* magazine in England. She serves as poetry editor for *Lilipoh* magazine and teaches poetry/writing workshops.

Perie Longo is the author of three poetry collections, most recently *With Nothing Behind But Sky: a journey through grief* (Artamo, 2006), and is widely published in journals and anthologies. She is a past president of the National Association for Poetry Therapy, a past Poet Laureate of Santa Barbara, and chair of the Nuclear Age Peace Foundation's poetry committee. A marriage and family therapist, she teaches with California Poets in the Schools and leads private poetry workshops. www.perielongo.com

Paula C. Lowe lives on a cattle ranch east of Arroyo Grande. Her most recent work can be found in *Askew, Dogwood, The Sow's Ear, Solo Café, New Times,* and *Poems For Endangered Places.* She is the managing editor of *Solo Novo* and Solo Press and a member of the Cambria Writers Workshop. Her nonfiction books include *CarePooling, HomeWorks,* and *Dolphin Kidkits.* She completed her graduate degree and fiction program at University of Washington.

Friday Lubina is assistant editor of *Askew Poetry Journal* and volunteers for the Ojai Raptor Rehabilitation Center. Since 1991, she has hosted and performed at poetry events throughout the state. Currently, she hosts "Friday on Saturday" at the Artists Union Gallery in Ventura on the last Saturday of every month. Her poems have appeared in *Caffeine, Art/Life Limited Editions, Dance of the Iguana,* and *Goodbye Gianna, Goodbye.*

Glenna Luschei is founder and publisher of *Solo Press* and author of many poetry books, among them *Witch Dance* (Presa Press, 2010), *Salt Lick* (West End Press, 2008), and a translation of Sor Juana Inés de la Cruz's *Enigmas* (Solo Press, 2006). She has received D. H. Lawrence and NEA fellowships, the Fortner Award, and an honorary doctorate from St. Andrews Presbyterian College. She was named Poet Laureate of San Luis Obispo in 2000.

Maia's poems and short fiction have appeared in many journals and anthologies, including *Askew* and *Lucid Stone.* She lives in Isla Vista and values nature and all its amazing denizens, political/economic justice, music, organic gardening, co-creative projects, and good conversations with good people, including her grown son and daughter. She is the author of *A Woman Green As the Sea* (Pieces of the Moon, 1991), and her book *The Spiritlife of Birds* is forthcoming from Askew.

Born in California, **devorah major** is the granddaughter of West Indian documented and undocumented immigrants. She is a poet, novelist, and internationally touring performer whose books include *black bleeds into green* (Word Temple Press, 2010) *where river meets ocean* (City Lights Foundation Books, 2003), *with more than tongue* (Creative Arts Book Company, 2003), *Brown Glass Windows* (Curbstone Press, 2002), and *An Open Weave* (Berkley, 1997). She served as Poet Laureate of San Francisco from 2002-2006.

Diane Kirsten Martin's work has appeared or is forthcoming in *Field, New England Review, Poetry Daily, Crazyhorse, Harvard Review,* and *Narrative.* She received second place in the Nimrod/Hardman Pablo Neruda Prize competition in 2004 and was included in *Best New Poets 2005.* She has received a Pushcart Special Mention and won the Erskine J. Poetry Prize from *Smartish Pace.* Her first collection, *Conjugated Visits,* was published in 2010 by Dream Horse Press.

Julianna McCarthy lives above the snow line, with a dog and two cats, in the Los Padres National Forest. She has received a first prize from *The Bridge,* the Schieble Sonnet Prize, and a Pushcart Prize nomination. Her chapbook *Photoplay* was released in 2009 by Finishing Line Press. Her poems have appeared in *The Antioch Review, Alehouse, 51%, Boxcar Poetry Review, Spot Lit,* and *Best Poem.* She holds an MFA in creative writing/poetry from New England College.

Kathleen McClung lives in San Francisco and teaches at Skyline College and the Writing Salon. Her poems, stories, and essays have appeared in *Bloodroot, Spirituality & Health, Poetry Now, Tule Review, Poetry Northwest, City Works, Poets 11 2010: An Anthology of Poems,* and elsewhere. She has received prizes from the Robert Frost Foundation, Sacramento Poetry Center, Soul-Making Literary Competition, SOMArts Cultural Center, Memoirs Ink, and the Academy of American Poets.

Deborah A. Miranda, associate professor of English at Washington and Lee University, is the author of *The Zen of La Llorona* (Salt Publishing, 2005); *Indian Cartography* (Greenfield Review Press, 1999), which won the First Book Award from the Native Writers' Circle of the Americas; and an unpublished collection titled *Raised By Humans.* She is a member of the Ohlone-Costanoan Esselen Nation of California. Her mixed-genre book, *Bad Indians: A Tribal Memoir,* is forthcoming from Heyday Books.

Charlotte Muse teaches and writes poetry in Menlo Park. Her recent awards include the Yeats Society of New York Poetry Award, two *Atlanta Review* International Publication Awards, and prizes in the Joy Harjo Poetry Award, the Friends of Acadia, and the Foley Prize competitions. A letterpress edition of her chapbook, *A Story Also Grows,* was handmade by Chester Creek Press in 2010. She likes to sit at the bottom of a nearby dry creek bed staring into space.

Carol Muske-Dukes has authored 13 books, including eight volumes of poetry. Her latest, *Twin Cities* (Penguin Poets Series), came out in June 2011. She is currently Poet Laureate of California; her statewide project, the Magic Poetry Bus, will produce a free online and print poetry handbook. Awards include Guggenheim and NEA fellowships, the Dylan Thomas Poetry Award, and the Library of Congress Award. She writes for *The New York Times, Los Angeles Times,* and *The Huffington Post.*

Jim Natal is the author of three poetry collections: *Memory and Rain* (Red Hen Press, 2009), *Talking Back to the Rocks* (Archer Books, 2003), and *In the Bee Trees* (Archer Books, 2000). A three-time Pushcart Prize nominee (2007–2009), his work has appeared in many literary journals and anthologies, including the recent *New Poets of the American West* and *Beyond Forgetting: Poetry and Prose About Alzheimer's Disease.*

Ruth Nolan, M.A, is Professor of English at College of the Desert, where she teaches California desert/Indian literature and creative writing. A native of the Mojave Desert and former BLM-California Desert District firefighter, she is also a writer and lecturer whose poetry and prose related to the California desert are widely published in literary journals and magazines. She is editor of *No Place for a Puritan: The Literature of California's Deserts* (Heyday Books, 2009).

David Oliveira is a native of California's San Joaquin Valley. He is the publisher and editor of Mille Grazie Press, inventor of Poet Cards, and founding editor of *Solo.* His books include *A Little Travel Story* (Harbor Mountain Press, 2008) and *In the Presence of Snakes* (Brandenburg Press, 2000). His poems have appeared widely in journals and anthologies. He now lives in Phnom Penh, Cambodia, where he teaches English at Pannásástra University.

Enid Osborn, co-editor of *A Bird Black As the Sun*, came to California in 1981. A native of New Mexico, she studied Latin American literature at UNM. She founded Green Poet Project in 1999 to produce readings and "lively-up the poetry scene" in Santa Barbara. Her work has appeared in four chapbooks and various journals, received a Billee Murray Denny award, and was nominated for a 2009 Pushcart Prize. An avid birder, she once sang with the group Bright Raven.

Melinda Palacio grew up in South Central Los Angeles and now lives in Santa Barbara. She holds two degrees in comparative literature and was a 2007 PEN Center USA Emerging Voices Fellow. Her work has appeared in a variety of publications. *Folsom Lockdown,* the 2009 winner of Kulupi Press's Sense of Place contest, is her first chapbook. Her first novel is *Ocotillo Dreams* (Bilingual Press, 2011). She is a Friday columnist on LaBloga.com

Robert Peake studied poetry at UC Berkeley and in the MFA program at Oregon's Pacific University. His poems have appeared in *Askew, California Quarterly, North American Review, Poetry International, Rattle,* and two anthologies of Southern California poetry. Until recently, he lived in Ojai with his wife, Valerie, and cat, Miranda. The family relocated to London, England in 2011. He writes about poetry on his website, www.robertpeake.com

Connie Post served as Poet Laureate of Livermore, California from 2005-2009. Her work has appeared in journals such as *Calyx, Kalliope, Cold Mountain Review, Chiron*

Review, Crab Creek Review, Comstock Review, DMQ Review, Dogwood, Main Street Rag, The Great American Poetry Show, Karamu, The Pedestal Magazine, RiverSedge, Up The Staircase, and *The Toronto Quarterly*. She received the 2009 Caesura Poetry Award from the Poetry Center of San Jose.

Peg Quinn has published poems in regional journals, is a 2010 Pushcart Prize nominee, won the 2010 Santa Barbara Symphony Poetry Contest, paints murals on commission, and is an art specialist at a private elementary school.

R. S. Read is a poet and writer living on California's Central Coast. His poetry has been published in several regional journals, including the literary magazine of De Anza College, *Red Wheelbarrow*. He has adopted Marvin Bell's advice: "You must write many, many bad words before you write any good ones."

Sojourner Kincaid Rolle is a poet, playwright, and peacemaker. Her poems have been published in six chapbooks and in various anthologies and literary magazines. She has been teaching young writers through her Song of Place Poetry Project since 1997. Her book *Black Street* was published by UC Santa Barbara's Center for Black Studies Research in 2009. She is a former advisory editor for *SageTrail* Poetry Magazine.

Halie Rosenberg is a writer/performer living in Los Angeles. She has performed her original work at venues such as The Improv, Upright Citizen's Brigade, Mbar, and Chi Chi's Word Parlor. Her flash fiction has received an award from Women On Writing. However, the pinnacle of her creative career can be defined as the time she portrayed a befuddled crow in Mac Wellman's *Crowtet: A Murder of Crows*.

Mary Rudge's books include *Hungary, Austria, and Other Passions* and *Passport Always Everywhere Poems* (Xlibris, 2010). She coordinated Oakland's first literary arts festival plus many other multimedia and multicultural events. A historian for the island of Alameda, she served as Alameda's first Poet Laureate and also as a board member of the California Federation of Chaparral Poets. She has traveled widely as an ambassador for poetry and peace with the World Congress of Poets.

Mary Kay Rummel's latest book of poetry is *What's Left Is The Singing* (Blue Light Press, 2010). Her other recent books include *Love in the End* (Bright Hill Press, 2008) and *The Illuminations* (Cherry Grove, 2006). A professor emerita of the University of Minnesota, she teaches part-time at California State University, Channel Islands and lives in Ventura. She has read her work at many venues in the U.S., Ireland, and England. http://marykayrummel.com

Kay Ryan was appointed the nation's 16th Poet Laureate in 2008. Her notable books include *The Best of It: New and Selected Poems* (Grove Press, 2010) and *Flamingo Watching* (Copper Beech Press, 1994). She has received the Ruth Lilly Poetry Prize, a Guggenheim fellowship, a National Endowment for the Arts fellowship, and three Pushcart Prizes. Raised in the San Joaquin Valley and the Mojave Desert, she has lived in Marin County for the past 40 years.

June Sylvester Saraceno is the author of *Altars of Ordinary Light*, a collection of poetry, and *Mean Girl Trips*, a chapbook. Her work has appeared in many journals, including *American Journal of Nursing, California Quarterly, Haight-Ashbury Literary Journal, The Pedestal, Silk Road, Smartish Pace, Tar River Poetry,* and *The Rambler*, as well as the anthologies *Passionate Hearts* and *Intimate Kisses*. She is chair of the English program at Sierra Nevada College and founding editor of *Sierra Nevada Review*.

Edwin Shaw is a mask maker, puppeteer, dancer, teacher, bodysurfer, and birdwatcher as well as a poet. His first novel in verse, *Larry's Rock,* was published in 2010 by Pelican Wind Press. He has also published numerous chapbooks of poetry. His passions include writing songs and playing the guitar. He cites Bob Dylan as the writer who turned him on to poetry and John Keats as his first poetry teacher. He lives in Santa Barbara.

Kim Shuck is a writer, artist, curator, frustrated mom, and recovering sarcastic. Her first solo book of poetry, *Smuggling Cherokee* (Greenfield Review Press, 2005) won the Diane Decorah Award from the Native Writers' Circle of the Americas. Her recent work has appeared in *New Poets of the American West* (Many Voices Press, 2010) and *I Was Indian* (FootHills Publishing, 2009). In 2010, she was awarded a co-residency at the de Young Museum in San Francisco.

Dian Sousa's books include *Lullabies for the Spooked and Cool* (Mille Grazie Press, 2005) plus *Sunday Blood and Jamaica Rum: Poems of Spiritual Schizophrenia* (Tabula Rasa Press). Her poems have been published in various journals, including *Prairie Schooner, Gavea Journal, Solo Café, Bakunin, Art/Life, Asylum,* and *Askew*.

Known mainly as a poet/teacher, **Barry Spacks** has brought out novels, stories, three poetry CDs, and 10 poetry collections. He has taught literature and writing for many years, first at Massachusetts Institute of Technology (1960-1981) and since then at UC Santa Barbara. His most recent book of poems, from Cherry Grove, is *Food for the Journey.*

Ann Stanford (1916-1987) published 11 poetry collections, a translation of the Bhagavad Gita, a collection of women's poetry, and two books on the poet Anne Bradstreet. She taught at California State University Northridge for over two decades and was the first woman in the CSU system to be named Outstanding Professor of the Year. Her poetry received numerous awards in her lifetime, and the University of Southern California created the Ann Stanford Poetry Prize in her honor.

David Starkey was the 2009-2011 Poet Laureate of Santa Barbara and directs the creative writing program at Santa Barbara City College. His poetry collections include *It Must Be Like the World* (Pecan Grove, 2011), *A Few Things You Should Know About the Weasel* (Biblioasis, 2010), *Starkey's Book of States* (Boson Books, 2007), and *Ways of Being Dead: New and Selected Poems* (Artamo, 2006). He has published over 400 poems in literary journals.

Born in Glendale, California, poet and translator **Joseph Stroud** was educated at the University of San Francisco, California State University Los Angeles, and San Francisco

State University. His poetry collections include *Signatures* (1982), *Below Cold Mountain* (1998), *Country of Light* (2004), and *Of This World: New and Selected Poems* (2008). He has received the Library of Congress's Witter Bynner Fellowship and a Pushcart Prize, and his work has been featured on The Writer's Almanac.

Patrice Vecchione is the author of a volume of poems, *Territory of Wind* (Many Names Press, 1999); a nonfiction book, *Writing and the Spiritual Life* (McGraw-Hill, 2001); and a one-woman play, *A Woman's Life in Pieces* (2009). She is also the editor of several poetry anthologies for young adults, including *Faith and Doubt* (Henry Holt, 2007). She teaches writing and collage workshops at Esalen Institute and elsewhere. Patrice lives in Monterey. www.patricevecchione.com

Doris Vernon has been associated with the poetry scene in Ventura County for more than 10 years, conducting a poetry workshop and reading her poems at various venues. She has published four chapbooks as well as a full-length collection titled *In Secluded Recesses* (Vernon Books, 2005). Along with her fellow-poets, she is mindful of the advice of Coleridge: "Try to use the best words in the best order."

A former psychology researcher and writer/editor, **Patricia Wellingham-Jones** has published poetry in many journals and Internet magazines, including *HazMat Review, Ibbetson Street, Edgz,* and *Wicked Alice.* She has a special interest in healing writing and writes for the review department of *Recovering the Self: a Journal of Hope and Healing.* She is the author of 10 chapbooks; *End-Cycle: Poems About Caregiving* won the Palabra Productions Chapbook Contest in 2006.

Jackson Wheeler was born and raised in North Carolina. He attended the University of North Carolina, Chapel Hill and graduate school in California where he has lived since 1975. He is the author of *A Near Country: Poems of Loss* (Solo Press, 1999), with Glenna Luschei and David Oliveira, and *Swimming Past Iceland* (Mille Grazie Press, 1993). He co-edited *SOLO: A Journal of Poetry* for 10 years.

Charan Sue Wollard was the 2009-2011 Poet Laureate of Livermore. Her poems have appeared in the *Carquinez Review, Literary Harvest,* and Las Positas anthologies. Her first book of poetry, *In My Other Life,* was released in 2010 by Richer Resources Publishing. She is a member of the Poet's Society and the Ina Coolbrith Poetry Circle. Her work has won numerous awards, including the Grand Prize at the 2004 California Poets' Dinner.

Cecilia Woloch is the author of five poetry collections, most recently *Carpathia* (BOA Editions, 2009) and *Narcissus* (Tupelo Press, 2006). She has taught poetry workshops for children and adults in the U.S. and abroad. She is currently a lecturer in creative writing at the University of Southern California and founding director of the Paris Poetry Workshop. The recipient of a 2011 NEA fellowship, she divides her time between Los Angeles, Atlanta, Paris, and southeastern Poland.

Acknowledgments

Maureen Alsop: "Cledonomancy, Sleep in the Raven's Throat" appeared in the online journal *Escape into Life,* www.escapeintolife.com, and is used by permission of the author.

Cynthia Anderson: "A Parable" appeared in *Askew,* Issue 8, Spring/Summer 2010 and is used by permission of the author.

Len Anderson: "On the Nature of Things" appeared in *Affection for the Unknowable* (Hummingbird Press, 2003) and is used by permission of the author.

Lisl Auf der Heide: "Black Birds" appeared in *Child of the Universe* (Lisl Auf der Heide, 2006) and is used by permission of the author.

M. L. Brown: "Wheatfield with Crows" appeared in *Ekphrasis,* Vol. 3 No. 6, Fall/Winter 2005 and is used by permission of the author.

Christopher Buckley: "Crows in Coatesville" appeared in *A Short History of Light* (Painted Hills Press, 1994) and is used by permission of the author.

Frances Pettey Davis: "Last Crow" appeared in *Askew*, Issue 8, Spring/Summer 2010 and is used by permission of the author.

ellen: A version of "Giving Birth to Ravens" appeared in *Inky Blue,* Issue 4, 1991 under a different title and is used by permission of the author.

William Everson: "These Are the Ravens" appeared in *These Are the Ravens* (Pamphlet Series of Western Poets), © 1935 by William Everson, and is used by permission of Jude Everson.

Paul Fericano: "Curly Howard Misreads Edgar Allan Poe" appeared in *Heavy Bear,* Issue 7, 2010 and *The Outlaw Poetry Network* (France), December 2010, and is used by permission of the author.

Lawrence Ferlinghetti: "In woods where many rivers run (#19)" appeared in *A Coney Island of the Mind*, © 1958 by Lawrence Ferlinghetti and is used by permission of New Directions Publishing Corp.

Mary Fitzpatrick: "Journey Through Night" appeared in *Askew*, Issue 8, Spring/Summer 2010 and is used by permission of the author.

Dan Gerber: "The Crow" appeared in *Trying to Catch the Horses* (Michigan State University Press, 1999) and is used by permission of the author.

Lara Gularte: "Finding the Sacred," winner of the Surprise Valley Poetry Prize, appeared in the *Modoc Independent News,* Vol. 6, Issue 5, May 2009 and is used by permission of the author.

Michael Hannon: "What the Crow Said" appeared in *Fables* (Turkey Press, 1988) and "Born Again" appeared in *Trusting Oblivion* (If Publishing, 2002) and are used by permission of the author.

Susan Kelly-DeWitt: "Confronting the Angel" appeared in *Feather's Hand* (Swan Scythe Press, 2000) and "Crows at Evening" appeared in *The Fortunate Islands* (Marick Press, 2008) and are used by permission of the author.

Kit Kennedy: "License to Travel" appeared in the *Saranac Review*, Issue 2, 2006 and is used by permission of the author.

Steve Kowit: "Raven" appeared in *The First Noble Truth* (University of Tampa Press, 2007) and is used by permission of the author.

Philip Levine: "The Three Crows" appeared in *THE MERCY: Poems by Philip Levine*, copyright © 1999 by Philip Levine and is used by permission of Alfred A. Knopf, a division of Random House, Inc.

Ellaraine Lockie: "Encounters with Crows" appeared in *Champion Poems* (England) as a contest finalist in the *Sentinel Literary Quarterly* Poetry Competition and is used by permission of the author.

Perie Longo: "Crows' Feet" appeared in *Lucid Stone*, Fall 1997 and is used by permission of the author.

Glenna Luschei: "Bird of Paradox" appeared in *Late Prayer* (Presa Press, 2011) and is used by permission of the author.

Kathleen McClung: "Nephew, Blurred" received an honorable mention in the 2010 Sacramento Poetry Center Contest, appeared in *Poetry Now* January-February 2011, and is used by permission of the author.

Carol Muske-Dukes: "Crows" appeared in *Washington Square Review* No. 23, 2009, and *Twin Cities* (Penguin Poets Series, 2011) and is used by permission of the author.

Jim Natal: "Lost: One-Footed Adult Crow. Reward." appeared in *Memory and Rain* (Red Hen Press, 2009) and "Early Morning Crow" appeared in *In the Bee Trees* (Archer Books, 2000) and are used by permission of the author.

Melinda Palacio: "disconcerted crow" appeared in *Pilgrimage Magazine*, Volume 35, Issue 3, Winter 2010 and is used by permission of the author.

Kay Ryan: "Paired Things" appeared in *Flamingo Watching*, © 1994 by Kay Ryan and is used by permission of Copper Beech Press.

Sojourner Kincaid Rolle: "The Pallbearers" appeared in *Common Ancestry* (Mille Grazie Press, 1999) and is used by permission of the author.

Edwin Shaw: "Crows" appeared in *The Boy Who Wanted to Fly* (Pelican Wind Press, 2009) and is used by permission of the author.

Gary Snyder: The epigraph for *A Bird Black As the Sun* is taken from "The swallow-shell that eases birth" (Hunting: 4) in *Myths & Texts*, © 1978 by Gary Snyder and is used by permission of New Directions Publishing Corp.

Barry Spacks: "The Strolling Crow" originally appeared in *The Carleton Miscellany,* was reprinted in *Something Human* (Harper's Magazine Press, 1972), and is used by permission of the author.

Ann Stanford: "The Committee" appeared in *The Descent,* © 1970 by Ann Stanford and is used by permission of Viking Penguin, a division of Penguin Group (USA) Inc.

Joseph Stroud: "Night in Day" appeared in *Of This World: New and Selected Poems 1966-2006,* © 1998 by Joseph Stroud, and is used by permission of The Permissions Company, Inc. on behalf of Copper Canyon Press, www.coppercanyonpress.org

Doris Vernon: "The Crow and the Artist" appeared in *RATTLE* #26 and is used by permission of the author.

Cecilia Woloch: "Lasswade, Midlothian: Dusk" appeared in *Late* (BOA Editions, 2003) and is used by permission of the author.

INDEX OF POETS

CPSIA information can be obtained at www.ICGtesting.com
Printed in the USA
LVOW040743271111

256574LV00002B/140/P

9 780615 536323